FUN & NAMES

OR HOW TO DIG YOUR FAMILY HISTORY WITHOUT REALLY PRYING

DISCLOSED BY
GEORGE D. DURRANT

UNDERCOVER WORK BY
NOEL R. BARTON

BOOKCRAFT

Salt Lake City, Utah

Library of Congress Catalog Card Number: 80-65244
ISBN O-88494-392-5

First Printing, 1980

Lithographed in the United States of America
PUBLISHERS PRESS
Salt Lake City, Utah

Contents

Introduction

You have just opened a very exciting "who done it" or "how to do it" book on heritage hunting. On these pages is the unfolding of a wonderful mystery — a mystery best encompassed by the question, "Who am I?"

Prompted by reminiscing about my old high school sweater, I began to dig into my past. Once again I saw my boyhood days back in my little town. I recalled again the cool front porch of my antique family home; the wooden airplanes which I carved with a pocket knife; the old weather-worn and sagging barn, the dark damp cellar; the country road that came from town to our place and then continued on to my friend Herbie Pawlowski's house; Allen's pond filled with pollywogs, a dozen different dogs, and the lilac tree.

Father and mother, now gone, came back ever stronger into my mind and heart. Grandparents and great-grandparents became not only my ancestors but my dear friends.

Prying into the past and finding the long-forgotten and almost lost memories has been like seeking clues in an intriguing mystery. And in so doing I've experienced thrills as difficult to describe as viewing a sunset or as falling in love. In the end, when all the clues were laid out into a long chain of evidence, I found an answer for my friends who have so often wondered about me. By digging right to the bottom of my family history, I finally found myself. I learned that my history plus my pedigree really equal me.

Of course, I couldn't have found what I did without help. Noel Barton, essentially the co-author of this book, was the detective who did all the undercover work to reveal clue after clue about my heritage. You who have done much searching into the ancestral past may already be acquainted with Noel. I asked a noted genealogist and historian if he knew Mr. Barton. He quickly replied, "Oh, yes indeed. I know Noel. He and I often frequent the same cemeteries."

Noel is among the foremost genealogists in America today. He is the "private genealogical eye" who guides and directs me and you as we read each of the following pages. He truly shows us the way to dig into our family history. He is the teacher. I the writer and you the reader are the students.

So if you are ready to be entertained, to laugh, to cry, to be inspired, and to find out how to learn about your family history, get your pick and shovel, pen and paper, camera and tape recorder, and your own private memory, and let's head off into the past. When we get to the other end of this book, and then when you've dug into your heritage, you will see yourself as you've never done before; and what you see could make you far more than you've ever been before.

There's an attic right above you and a trunk over in the corner. So let's get on with it. Keep your eyes wide open. The mystery surrounding your family is about to be disclosed.

1 *The Red Sweater*

I reached for my shirt, looked down the long line of hangers, and saw a white piece of clothing. I pulled it out from among the many bits of apparel. It was Marilyn's old high school sweater. The year was printed on the side near the pocket. For reasons of personal safety, I cannot recall now just what that year was. A red block letter *E* added to the beauty of this most significant piece of clothing.

I held the sweater in my hand and hurried to the front room where Marilyn was dusting. "Hey, look what I've got!" I shouted with enthusiasm. "It's your old school sweater."

With a slight tone of hostility she replied, "It's not old."

I gulped. "Of course not, but where has it been? I haven't seen it in the closet before."

"It's been in my cedar chest," she replied.

"I wonder where my old sweater is. I haven't seen it for a long time."

"Neither have I. It's so old it has probably decayed and turned to dust." At that she laughed a little.

A bit hurt, I returned to the closet and made a quick search, but, like a pessimistic archaeologist, I knew I wouldn't find it. I longingly whispered aloud, "Oh, if only I had owned a cedar chest!"

The next morning as I began to shave, I remembered again how much that red sweater had meant to me. In my mind I vividly recalled the day when I was first measured for that fine garment. The year was 1948; it was near the end of my junior year in high school. As the school day wore on, I was called from a math class and told to report to the office. You can imagine how upset I was at having to leave something as thrilling as a math class on a spring afternoon.

Walt Devey, the owner of Devey's Men's Store, was in the office waiting for me. While holding a tape measure in his hand, he announced, "Okay, George, let's measure you for your school sweater."

As he put the tape this way and that way, I tried to stand tall and to sort of puff out my chest. In spite of these efforts, he quietly noted, "You're not nearly as big as your older brother, are you?"

"Not quite," I replied regretfully, while wishing that I was.

Finally, Mr. Devey was finished and all the data was recorded. "That will do it, George. You'll get your sweater when you come back to school in September.

Summer came and was gone, and then it was fall. After a few weeks of my senior year, I arrived at school one day and had just about reached my locker when I was told that the sweaters had arrived. I excitedly put my books in my locker and, as I closed the door and turned around, I saw a friend who already had his. It was beautiful! Printed near the side pocket was the year: "1949," and there were some white stripes on the arm. As I gazed at the letter *A* I wanted to stand, place my hand over my heart, and sing the school song:

> Dear old American Fork High.
> Yes, we will love you till we die.
> Your banners bright, all red and white,
> Will be a beacon through the night.

However, there wasn't time for such glorious verse, for I had a date with destiny. I hurried to the office with almost wild anticipation. After sorting through several sweaters, Mr. Devey responded, "Oh, yes, here's yours."

The time had come. There before my eyes was my school sweater. With hands trembling, I put first one arm in and then the other. Then I stopped. Something was wrong. The ends of the sleeves were nearly at my elbows. I could hardly pull it around me tight enough to button it. My heart sank, and I shouted, "Hey, this isn't mine; it's too small!"

Mr. Devey quietly checked his records and announced, "It's yours all right."

Inwardly I concluded, *I can't wear this sweater*. Instant agony entered into my soul. You and I know that tough seniors don't cry, but I nearly did.

Sensing my chagrin, Mr. Devey, one of the kindest, most generous men I've ever known, smiled. "I guess I made some mistakes on those measurements." I felt a little better as he added, "Let's measure you again." As he did so he commented softly, "You are about the same size as your brother." When he said that, the fact flashed into my mind that Mr. Devey hadn't erred in his measurement. The truth was that I had grown four inches during that hot summer of 1948. As I left school that day, I didn't have a sweater. But someday soon I would. I was happy.

A few weeks later my priceless sweater arrived, and it fit me to a tee. I really looked sharp when I wore it. For several years I wore it with pride.

These refreshing thoughts of days gone by had lasted an entire shave. I put aside the razor and began to comb my hair. "That was a long time ago—1949," I declared softly to myself. Funny, I still look the same as I did then. The other guys are getting older, but I still look the same. Oh, my hair's not quite as thick, and I've sagged a little, but I still look like my old 1949 senior self."

Again I looked deep into the mirror, and as I gazed into my own eyes a wonderful warm feeling entered into my entire soul. I fairly tingled for a few seconds as I was flooded with what seemed like a thousand memories of yesteryear. So many things had happened to me in the days that had been my past.

Somehow I could see a reflection of all those things in my face, and I could feel the effect that each experience had had on my heart.

Stimulated by my memories, I softly said to the reflection in the mirror: "That face is not original with me. It was not shaped by my victories or defeats or joys or sorrows alone. That face was born before I ever drew a breath. That classic nose is far more prominent than I am. It began with my great-grandfather, or was it his father or his? My brown eyes were colored by my grandmother or her mother or hers. My ears, which brought me some fame as a child, were probably developed by ancestors who had once hoped to fly.

"My height came from my mother and her tall father and his. They are the ones Walt Devey should blame for having to make me two sweaters for the price of one.

"Yes," I said to myself, "there I am in the mirror, but I am not really just me. I am made up of my own personal and peculiar blend of an ancestral reservoir: a little bit of him and a touch of her and a sprinkling of him and quite a dose of her, all of whom lived one, two, and even twenty generations ago.

"Did my dear ancestors ever, in a moment of vision, see my reflections in their mirror as I, in a moment of memory, can see them in mine?" As my mind was moving backward, the hands of the clock moved ahead. It was time for breakfast, and the past was gone. The bus would be too if I didn't get a move on.

2   *Enter the Detective*

All reflections of the old red sweater were gone as I hurried out of the house to catch the bus. As I rode along, my mind again became susceptible to the past. It was almost as if my memories came running down the street behind me. When the bus halted at the next stop, my memories got on with me—and because every seat was taken they sat right down in my heart. All the way to work those memories seemed to cry out for recognition by shouting, "Find out more, find out more!"

At work I told my friend Noel about my memories. After I had told him about my old red sweater, I commented, "I'd sure like to do some of—what do you call it? Gene— something."

"You mean genealogy?" he asked.

I almost shouted, "Yeah, genealogy, that's it! I want to do some genealogy!" However, my enthusiasm soon waned as I realized, "But Noel, I don't know how to even begin."

"I'll help you," he calmly answered.

That's how it all began.

Noel explained that heritage hunting was his main interest in both his professional life and in his leisure time. He is a pedigree and personal-history detective. He can uncover mysteries about the past that time had thought it had securely hidden forever.

Nearly every time we met during the time Noel and I began to work together, Noel would tell me something about his great-grandfather, Christopher Layton. One day he said with a smile on his face, "Christopher is both my great-grand-father and my great-great-grandfather."

"How could that be?" I asked.

"I'll tell you that later," he replied. "First let me tell you that he was born in Thorncote, England, on the eighth of March, 1821. His family was so poor that they were on church welfare. From that humble beginning he lived a life that led him from England to America, a life that didn't end until after he had become one of the richest and most powerful men on the western frontier of the United States.

"What do you think of that?" Noel asked proudly.

"I'm deeply impressed," I replied in awe. "He must have been an amazing man," I quickly added. "But what I can't understand is how could he have been both your great-grand-father and also your great-great-grandfather? That seems impossible."

"I'll explain that later, but listen to this." Noel's excitement grew. "Christopher never did learn to read or write, but because of his great power as a leader he became the president of an educational institution that later became a university."

I was a bit shocked. "That's amazing, but I still wonder how he could be both—"

Noel interrupted my question. "And he also was at Sutter's Fort right after gold was discovered. He didn't like mining, but he did like gold. So he went some miles to the south, bought horses for one and a half dollars a head, brought them back to the gold fields, and there he sold them to the gold miners for one hundred dollars in gold dust each."

"Quite a businessman," I admired. "But how could one man be both—"

Christopher Layton

Again Noel interrupted. "I'll say he was a businessman. He helped found a railroad, was on the board of directors for one of the West's leading department stores, and owned a freight company."

I pleaded, "But Noel, how could he be both—"

Noel broke in and added, "He once killed a buffalo with a pistol, and he had a nearly photographic memory."

As Noel paused, I jumped in, "But Noel, what I really want to know is how could—"

Again he interrupted me. "I know what you really want to know and I'll answer your question now. What you really want to know is why I know so much about this great man. Is that it?"

"Well, yes," I agreed, with the tone of one who has given up hope. I then added, "That's what I was really wondering."

Noel was now in a most talkative mood. "I got interested in Christopher Layton many years ago when I found out that he was my double ancestor."

Now it was my turn to interrupt. "How could—"

Noel didn't hear me. He continued without stopping. "Christopher couldn't write, and so he left no journal or history. But he did tell his story to several of his sons and his daughters, who wrote some of it down. However, there were large gaps in that history, and there were many important things which were left out. When I realized that the story was far from complete, I decided to go to work and find out everything I could about my great— I mean my great-great-grandfather."

Noel paused at this point, and I seized a chance to get in a word. "You told me he was your double ancestor. How—"

But that was as far as I could get. Noel broke in. "Are you about to inquire how I proceeded to learn more about him?"

I shrugged. "Yeah, how did you do it?"

He was off again. "Well, I read all the journals I could find which were written by men who knew him. They often wrote about him. That's how I found out about the story of his killing a buffalo with a pistol. I also went to the library and read every issue of the *Deseret News* from 1850 to 1880."

"Wow!" I exclaimed. "That's thirty years' worth of newspapers! That must have taken you a considerable amount of time."

"Yes, it did. For several months I would go to the library every morning at five o'clock and read until I had to go to work at eight, and so it wasn't all that difficult." Without pausing, Noel continued. "On one occasion we got Christopher's living daughters together and had them tell what they could recall about their father."

"That's a good idea," I offered.

"Well, it was until they began arguing over the details of a certain story," Noel chuckled. "It really got to be a bit of a squabble. I got up and left the room. After things had cooled down, I returned and visited with each of them — but only one at a time.

"After searching for years I was finally able to find ten different photographs of Christopher," Noel continued. "I believe that I now have every picture that was ever taken of him."

"Could I see the pictures?" I asked with eagerness.

"Sure," Noel replied, as he pulled a book from a shelf and showed me the priceless pictures, one by one.

"It really gets me excited to find out about my ancestors," I commented.

Noel raised his voice. "Speaking of excitement, listen to this. I learned of an old lady who had some old documents in her attic that I believed might include some of Christopher's business papers. I called on her in her nineteenth-century home, and she led me to the entrance of her attic. She then pointed inside. 'The papers are in there.' You can imagine my excitement. I could hardly hold the flashlight steady. It was like a gold mine. I sat on an old chair near an old trunk and some old clothes as I looked through the old books and papers."

As Noel told me this story, I could see that he was describing what to him was a most heavenly place and a glorious experience. His face fairly shone as he described the papers that he had found.

Noel then changed the scene. "I also visited my mother's cousin. She had two of the ten photos I just showed you, but she didn't even know she had them until I visited her."

Without pausing, Noel continued, "I've also read history books and letters and—"

I looked at my watch and interrupted Noel by saying, "I've got to go to lunch. Can you join me?"

"Not today," Noel replied. "I've got to do some more work on Christopher."

I gulped. "You mean you haven't finished yet after all these years and knowing all you've just told me?"

"Oh, no, there are still many things to learn and many mysteries to clear up before I can write the book."

"The book?" I questioned.

"Yes, the book. All of Christopher's ten thousand descendants are waiting."

"Ten thousand!" My tone showed my amazement.

"That's right, ten thousand."

"How could one man have so many descendants?" I asked.

"Well, it ties in with what I told you about his being my double ancestor. You see, it's like this—"

With great regret, I had to interrupt him. "Boy, I hate to leave because I think you were about to tell me the answer to my question. But I'm late. I'll be back again, and you can tell me then." I hurried off to a luncheon appointment murmuring, "Double ancestor, great-grandfather and great-great-grandfather?"

3   *Clues for the Asking*

T he morning sun had not yet appeared over the Wasatch Mountains when I arrived at Noel's home. He had agreed to go with me to my old hometown to help me find clues about my past. I rang the bell and was invited in. For a few moments Noel finished some chores, and I sat alone in his front room. I was anxious to talk to him, for my first question was going to be, "How could Christopher be both your great- and your great-great-grandfather?" As I looked around, my eyes froze on a certain piece of furniture. I couldn't believe what I was seeing. There, near the couch, was a short-legged table, and the top of the table—no it couldn't be. I stood up and took two steps and looked down. It was what I had thought it was: a large, flat gravestone.

As I looked silently in disbelief, Noel entered and stood behind me. I jumped as he asked, "How do you like it?"

"How did you get that?" I wondered.

"It belonged to my fourth great-grandfather, Thomas Taylor Owsley," Noel explained.

"Oh," I said, as I read that same name engraved on the beautiful piece of white sandy marble. "Did Thomas give it to you, or did you have to take it over his dead body?"

"Some years ago I found a picture of Thomas Taylor Owsley in an old trunk. I was fascinated by him, and I determined to learn more about his life. I knew he lived in Kentucky, but I didn't know where. I knew he was born in 1776, but I had no idea when he died or where. By reading some old letters I discovered that during the last years of his life he lived in Hickman County.

"I finally had the opportunity to go to that area. I searched the county records and read copies of the old newspapers. I talked with people in town to locate relatives, but I couldn't find any. I also studied the tax records at the Kentucky Historical Society. Finally, I learned that Thomas had lived and eventually died a mile outside of Clinton. I went to this small town, because I had an intense desire to find his grave.

"It was Saturday when I entered Clinton. I really didn't know how to find the old Owsley family cemetery that people had told me about. As I was thinking about how I might proceed, I saw a very old home. For a moment I forgot the cemetery and decided to photograph that house. As I stood in the road facing the home, an elderly lady came hobbling out and waved at me in a somewhat frantic manner. At first I thought she was upset because of my photographic activities, but then I could tell she was beckoning me to the door.

"As I approached she asked, 'What do you want?'

"I told her I was interested in taking a picture of her antebellum home and was also looking for the old Owsley cemetery. I needed to find someone who might know where it was located.

" 'Come in and talk to my husband,' she beckoned. 'He's the oldest living man in town.'

"I entered and had a most interesting talk with him. As we conversed, I mentioned Thomas Owsley to him and described the appearance of the tombstone that I was seeking. I told him exactly what it looked like. He asked, 'Have you been there before and seen the stone?'

" 'No, I haven't seen it before, but somehow I know what it looks like.'

" 'From your description I know the tombstone you are seeking,' he offered. 'I know right where it is.'

" 'When I was twelve,' he continued, 'I used to go to that cemetery each week with a friend to help him put flowers on his mother's grave. I remember seeing the tombstone you are searching for.'

"My excitement was intense as I listened. I eagerly interjected, 'Where is that cemetery?'

"He told me to go down the road some nine-tenths of a mile, and he concluded by saying, 'There on the right, amidst a clump of trees you will find it.' I thanked him and hurried to my car to begin the short journey that would lead me to the place that I desired to see.

"When I had driven the small distance, I was deeply disappointed to see that even though the place was a cemetery the grave markers were no longer visible. I walked into the center of the area and began to walk back and forth. After a search of several minutes, I found a small rectangular stone. I picked it up and could see that it was a footmarker. A thrill surged through me as I read the weatherworn letters: T.T.O. I said softly, 'Thomas Taylor Owsley.' Now I knew that I was in the right place, and my enthusiasm again flamed up within me. A further search soon brought back my discouragement, for I could find nothing else.

"Finally, in desperation I went to the nearby house. I knocked on the door, and, after greeting the man who answered, I told him about my search. He most graciously returned with me to the cemetery. As we walked about, kicking away at the weeds which covered the ground, he said, 'The man who now owns this property used some of the tombstones in a corral to serve as stepping stones for his cattle, but before he did that there was a feller from a nearby town who copied each of the tombstone inscriptions.' He suggested that perhaps this man could help me.

"I thanked him for his help and headed back to find the man he had described. I finally found the man. He was one of those wonderful people who sensed the sacredness and importance of such historical data and had thus copied the tombstone inscriptions. He told me that he remembered well the very tombstone I sought. As I departed, he said, 'Search just a little north of the center of the lot and you will find it.'

"I returned to the cemetery as quickly as I could this time. I borrowed a pitchfork from the man I had talked to before. He and I began to probe through the honeysuckle-covered rich black soil. It was a warm, humid Kentucky afternoon. As I probed the earth, sweat began to form on my forehead. After some minutes, the prongs of the fork struck a solid object. I dug frantically with the fork and with my hands. I've never had more energy or strength. The two or three inches of soil were soon pushed aside. I lifted up the dirt-covered stone. I brushed it off with my hand. I scarcely breathed as I read—first Thomas, then T, then Owsley. I had found a treasure which to me was much more precious than gold.

"The stone was broken in half, but within an inch of the place where I had found the first portion I found the other part. The stone was inscribed: 'born 29 April 1776; died 6 October 1860, Aged 84 yrs. 5 ms. 7 ds.'

"I carried the two stone treasures to the neighbor's lawn and washed them with water from his hose. He was most gracious as he said, 'If it is your ancestor, you had best take it with you or it will surely be lost forever.'

"I placed it in my car and drove to Paducah. There I had it crated at a monument works so that it could be shipped home.

"A week later when it was delivered, I wasn't home. The delivery man asked my wife, 'Where do you want this?'

'Just set it here by the back door and I'll move it later,' she explained.

" 'Well, you'd better decide where you want it because it is as heavy as h__ and you won't be able to move it once I set it down.'

"That evening when I returned home from work, my wife, Pam, told me that the stone had arrived. She told me what the delivery man had said about its weight. As I attempted to move it, I sensed what he meant. It was heavy, but to me it was as heavy as heaven. In the days that followed, I

Thomas Taylor Owsley

Gravestone of Thomas Taylor Owsley

had my brother make a frame and legs to place it in — and there it is."

I was speechless. Before Noel had told me this amazing story, I had considered the table to be beautiful. But now that I had heard how it came to be, it suddenly seemed sacred.

Noel added, "Remember, I told you that long before I found it I had seen it in my mind? Well, when I finally washed it off on that man's lawn, I saw that it was exactly the way I had pictured it."

Sensing his sincerity, I replied, "That sounds like a miracle."

"You bet it's a miracle. There are a lot of miracles that happen when you go looking for your ancestors. So let's go get in the car and head for American Fork and look for memories and ancestors." In a few minutes we were headed toward that very place — my old hometown.

I had been raised in that beautiful little city nestled on the northern shore of Utah Lake and guarded by the lofty peaks of Mount Timpanogos. However, years had gone by since I had moved away. I had returned many times to visit relatives, but never had I been as excited about going home as I was this day.

My excitement was like that which I had experienced as a boy as we watched our movie-hero private eyes search for each of the important clues of a case. Again I was on the edge of my seat, anxious to discover the solution to the mystery.

You see, Noel and I were truly going sleuthing. We were looking for Durrants, not live ones, but ones who had once lived. We were seeking the pieces of the puzzle hidden by time that could give us a clear picture of their lives.

As we journeyed down the highway, I eagerly pushed down the gas pedal until we were zooming along at fifty-five miles an hour.

By now we were at a place which is called the Point of the Mountain by the local citizens. As I looked out to my right, I could see the Utah State Prison. I felt as I always do when going by this forlorn place, that I was glad to be free. Little did I realize, at that time, that before my genealogical search had taken me back four generations, the records in that prison would reveal some hidden secrets about my great-grandfather.

As we passed by Lehi, a town adjacent to American Fork, I anticipated, "Noel, we will soon be there. What will we do first? Where will we go?"

"The problem is that we only have eight hours, so we can't come close to finishing all that we should do. If we really did the job right, it would take at least a week." He then added, "I'd like to stay here at least that long."

I looked at Noel, but he looked straight ahead. I thought to myself, *He wishes he could spend a whole week in my old hometown. He truly is a wise and wonderful man.*

"A week?" I asked. "What would we do if we spent an entire week here?"

"First we would make a list of all the people who knew your parents, grandparents and great-grandparents. Then we would visit them one by one and ask them to tell us about your people. We would take notes or tape-record the information which they could tell us. Some of these people would also have photos, documents, correspondence, and other things that would include your ancestors. They might even have some old journals and diaries that would mention some past Durrants."

"What else would we do?" I inquired.

"We'd visit the churches where they attended and look at the minutes of the meetings, membership records, and other church records. We would visit all the old businesses which have been in the community for a long time."

"Why would we do that?"

"Because they have financial records of things bought and sold. They might have minutes of the meetings of their board of directors. Perhaps the Durrants did business with them."

"Chipman's Store has been in American Fork for years," I remembered. "I'll bet they would have something. My dad used to go in there almost every day."

"They'd have something all right, but sometimes you can go to a place like that and ask them about their old records and they will say they don't have any. But if you prod them, they'll remember. It is best to talk to the employee who has worked in the store the longest.

"We would also visit all the fraternities and clubs such as the Masons, the Elks and the Lions or the local literary club," Noel continued.

"I don't think my people belonged to any of those."

"Well, you never really know until you check it out. We would also visit the banks, the drugstores, the grocery stores, the post office and the taverns."

"The taverns!" I exclaimed.

He smiled. "Well, maybe we could skip those.

"We would visit all the older schools in the town and the office of the school board. A most important visit would be to the local newspaper office. They should have copies of all their papers from the beginning."

"It would take a long time to read all of those," I responded.

"Yes, it would." But we would only read the local gossip sections; that's where the best things are. Of course, the obituaries are a gold mine of information such as death dates, other living relatives, and a brief history of the person's life. If the newspaper office doesn't have all the old newspapers, we could find them in public libraries and possibly on microfilm."

I could tell Noel was going to go on and on with suggestions of what we could do, but I interrupted him by shouting: "There it is, Noel! We are here. This is American Fork. This is my hometown. Let's stop and have a moment of silence."

"That's a great idea," Noel sympathized. "But we've only got eight hours, so full speed ahead."

Soon we were driving into the heart of downtown American Fork. "Should we go right to my brother Stewart's house?" I asked.

Noel thought for a second or two. "Yes, let's pick him up. He's older than you. You always want to get older people to help on a search like this. He will remember more about your people than you will, and he can show us things we will need to know."

As we drove through the business district, the fact that I was looking back in time caused me to see the stores and businesses all in a different way. I wasn't seeing them as they were now, but as they had been when I was a boy.

Now I rode down the streets of my hometown, seeing the past tracks of my boyhood, of my parents, my grandparents and on back. This city was now and had long been the home of a complete colony of Durrants.

When we arrived at his home, Stewart was as excited as I was. Friends are nice, but only brothers and sisters have the same heritage—and when you seek out that common past with them it binds you together in a bond of almost perfect love.

As we planned our day, Noel the detective directed, "First we will go to the cemetery."

"The cemetery?" I was surprised.

"Sure; this cemetery," Noel pointed out, "like the one in Kentucky, is full of clues about the past."

We drove to the cemetery. Noel took a quick look around. "This is probably quite a small cemetery, so even if you two didn't know where the graves were we could walk around for awhile and we would find them. If it were a bigger one we could get a map at the sexton's office or at the city hall."

I felt I had to set him straight. "American Fork is pretty big, Noel."

He smiled. "Yes, I suppose it could be compared to Clinton, Kentucky."

"Come on, Noel, American Fork is larger than Clinton."

"Yes, I guess you're right. Anyway, this is a city cemetery, and the one in Clinton was a small family one. Such cemeteries used to be and still are located all over, but we don't know where they are. The other day I found an old piece of a grave marker in my back yard, so I suppose someone is buried somewhere under my zucchini patch."

As we parked and walked inside the peaceful, well-kept, sacred place, Noel spoke softly. "We can find all sorts of things here."

"Like what?" I wondered.

"Names, parents, spouses, death dates and places and marriage dates."

As I walked along I found myself trying to read each verse on each stone.

"Sometimes there are verses that have some meaning in the person's life." Noel smiled as he recalled and repeated one he had read:

Here I be outside the church door.
Here I be because I'm poor.
The further in, the more they pay,
But here I be as snug as they.

That thought caused us to laugh a little, even in the cemetery. This encouraged Noel to offer another:

Here lies the body of Jonathan Peas,
Under the sod and under the trees.
But here you will find only the pod,
Peas shelled out, gone home to God.

This one was amusing, but it was also sacred—so we smiled but didn't laugh.

We were coming ever closer to my ancestors' graves. Noel continued his teaching. "It was on a tombstone that I found a real clue to an important part of the life of my great-grandfather, Albert A. Reneer. He worked on riverboats on the Green River in Kentucky. On his gravestone was a symbol that indicated he was a Mason. I wrote to the grand lodge and found out when he was admitted to the Masons and even when he died. I later found a picture of the Masons in Rochester, Kentucky, and—sure enough—there he was."

As we walked along looking, I commented, "I could spend the entire day here just looking and learning. All of these names bring back memories."

Stewart agreed. "Yes, I'm to the point where I have more friends here than I have downtown."

Upon hearing that comment, Noel explained, "Some people do spend days in cemeteries and even months. The Daughters of the American Revolution and others go into cemeteries and copy all the information down so that it can be preserved in libraries, historical societies, and other places."

Finally we were there. Stewart arrived first and exclaimed, "Here they are!" The sun was on our backs as we stood looking down at the grave sites of my beloved mother and father. For a few seconds we were all silent. Then Noel instructed, "Copy all the words and dates on the stones." As we did this, he took photographs of the tombstones which would also show all of the valuable information. He advised us that if we could we should always have a camera on such searches.

As we looked at the death dates, I recalled the funerals vividly. Then all sorts of memories started flowing into my mind. I didn't want to move on, but Noel prodded. "Come on, let's look for other Durrants." With some reluctance, I moved away from what seemed like a million wonderful memories.

After a short walk, Stewart declared in a voice loud enough to bring our scattered search party back into a close group, "Here's one!"

It was my grandfather's and grandmother's gravestone. What a thrill it was to see it! What was happening to me? Why would seeing a gravestone be so exciting? All I know is that I was thrilled. Birth to death—but what happened in between? I found myself resolving to find out.

The search went on. "Look at this!" shouted Noel. "John Durrant, and not one but two wives."

"Two wives!" I was amazed. Could this be my great-grandfather? Why were there two wives, both living at the same time?

The future search was going to be truly exciting, and this man who lay beneath this ground was going to become my personal hero.

"Which of the wives was my great-grandmother? Noel, we've got to find out about this man and these women."

"Calm down, George. We'll find out, but we must take it one step at a time," Noel calmly assured.

Flour or grist mill in Kaysville, Utah, representative of those used in 1895

The morning was half gone as we drove away from the cemetery. There was the old Star Flour Mill. We drove past it and then turned south down the beautiful mill lane. It did not seem to wind as much as it had in my boyhood days.

I drove slowly down this picturesque lane, and for a moment I forgot that I was with Noel and Stewart. In my mind I was walking down that lane again as I had done at least a thousand times as I grew up. I pictured the pleasant creek that parallels the lane. I remembered the small trout that I used to see each day as I walked home from school. As I crossed the bridge and gazed into the clear swirling water in the creek, I wondered if by now that small friend of so long ago had any great-grandfish swimming in those cool waters.

After driving a block or two further, we were out of the lane. There to the right, across the creek and up the hill, was dear old American Fork High School. Oh, the memories of this place! On we went to downtown American Fork.

Noel planned that the city hall would be our second stop. Ray Nelson, the city recorder, was most pleased to see us, as he was a long-time friend and a second cousin to both Stewart and me. We explained to him that we were in American Fork on a heritage hunt. Soon he was almost as interested in our efforts as we were.

He led us to a room where we could be seated at a table, and then at Noel's request he brought us the cemetery records. We spent more time than we should have with Ray, but we were talking about the old days and about people who had gone on before. We were having such a pleasant time that it was hard to hurry. Many names on the records were not relatives, but they reminded us of American Fork and the past.

Eventually we discovered an entry about mother, then father, then grandfather and grandmother, and finally great-grandfather and great-grandmother. There were dates and causes of deaths. It was like detective work. Each date gave us the thrill of finding a missing piece of the puzzle.

When we departed, we had copied several entries including these:

> [My great-grandfather]
> John Durrant born 28 April 1837, in England
> Father: William Durrant
> Mother: Mary Stewart
> Died 6 May 1914, of superlative gastria, in American
>   Fork

> [My great-grandmother]
> Elizabeth Jane Durrant born 17 September 1854,
>   Kings Langley, Hertfordshire
> Died 18 February 1931, Salt Lake City
> Accute paricarddites—grey casket—cement vault

We concluded our search in the city hall and said goodbye to Ray. It was almost noon. I looked at my watch. "Where has the morning gone?"

Noel's only answer was, "Let's hurry and go to your old family home."

To get there we drove up what used to be called the "Alpine Road." There is a new Alpine Road now, but we took the old one. It starts in downtown American Fork by the tabernacle and leads north to Third North, where it turns at Francis Abel's house. It continues east one block and turns north on Lizzie Steggle's corner. Then it leads straight north to Alpine.

As we rode along in silence, I thought, "Oh, the hundreds of times I've walked or ridden my bike down this old Alpine Road to get to and from the Cameo Theater." My brother Kent and I would go to every change of the movies and enjoyed such shows as a Roy Rogers, Hopalong Cassidy double feature. I had many memories scattered all along that old country road.

On Seventh North we saw our old home. Houses have now crowded the area, but that is not the way it used to be. We used to have plenty of space in which to roam.

The smell of Ashby's old place was now gone because the three-acre fox farm had long since become only a memory. I told Noel, "Right there is where the fox farm was. People would come and visit us and say, 'How can you stand to live in the stink of that fox farm?' I never did know what they were talking about because I had lived there for so long that I thought the air was supposed to hold such fragrance."

Noel took a picture of our old home. Later we learned that the neighbors had called the police because they didn't know who we were or what we were doing.

Our home looked different now than it did when we lived there. It had been remodeled and was now quite modern-looking. It was constructed many years ago of mud blocks which were called adobe. We had long since covered the adobe with plaster. When we did that, we thought that it had become more beautiful. As I looked at it with my memory, I could see the way it used to be—and the way it used to be was beautiful.

All of the chicken coops were gone now. We used to have four huge coops where we kept over two thousand chickens. My dad raised them for a living.

I was reminiscing. "Noel, I used to gather eggs three times a day and clean out the coops on Saturday morning!"

Noel asked me if I had written down all the things I was telling him.

I told him I hadn't. "Get busy and do it," he countered. "That is your life story; every person should write his story. If you really want to know your ancestors, you must first take your own life back to its beginning. After that, you can really come to know your ancestors."

I became excited about following Noel's instructions. I had so many memories. I knew I really should write them down. Noel, Stewart, and I agreed that everyone should make sure they leave a written or tape-recorded life history behind when they die.

I shouted, "Hey, Noel, why don't we get a law passed saying a person can't die until he has written his personal history?"

Noel chuckled. "Practice what you preach."

Our next stop was the old Harrington Elementary School. I could hardly enter the hallway because it was so crowded with memories. I almost shouted, "There is the very room where I attended the first grade. Let's see, my teacher's name was . . . I can't remember. But there is the room where I sat when I finally got fifteen out of twenty spelling words correct —an all-time high for me."

As we walked up the hall and down the stairs I continued to remember. "Hey, Noel, there is the cafeteria where I spilled my three-cent school lunch which consisted of a bowl of tomato soup. I hated to spill it, but that seemed better than eating it. School lunches in those days were not the delicious morsels the kids get today." Noel and Stewart both agreed.

"There is the area where they tried to teach me to dance. I could have done it, but the girls frightened me too badly."

Noel asked the secretary if there were any old school records in the building. She replied that there were. Noel suggested we look at them. I became nervous. "What if Noel finds out I have not always been the bright, alert student I am now?"

My fears were unfounded. I was brighter than I had remembered; I had received mostly *C* grades. Then I saw there before my very eyes the names of each of my teachers. So much was coming back to me now. I could write volumes about what went on within those walls and on the playground and behind the dance hall just across the street (where we used to go to fight).

I remembered my appointment there. At lunch I had had an argument with a classmate. We decided to settle it behind the dance hall after school. The fellow student didn't show up, and I've been grateful ever since. I was scared, but I guess he was too.

Time made us leave the school. It is strange what time does to us. It is fun to fly in the face of time by turning it backward against itself and dreaming again of the past.

Our next stop, scheduled by Noel, was the mortuary. The Anderson Mortuary used to be downtown. It was right on our route to the Cameo Theater. I remembered how I hated to pass that place at night. I was just grateful that I didn't have to pass the cemetery too, especially after some of the scary mummy shows.

However, the mortuary location had now changed. So much of my old hometown had moved and shifted. We soon arrived at the new location. Warren Anderson, Jr., greeted us warmly. We asked to see his records of the past. He wasn't quite sure what records he had. We went downstairs. Noel always knew just what to ask for. Soon we were looking at some old journals which contained some most fascinating facts. We found the following entries:

> William Albert Durrant [my grandfather]
> Charge to Durrant Brothers
> Date of Funeral: March 4, 1923
> Funeral Services: 1st Ward
> Burial Certificate No.: 10
> Death Date: March 1, 1923
> Occupation: Common Labor
> Birth Date: Oct. 30, 1870
> Age: 52 years, 4 months, 1 day
> Father: John Edward Durrant (England)
> Mother: Elizabeth J. Miller (England)
> Cost:
> $210.00 casket
>   28.00 clothing
> $238.00 total funeral

We also found a record of my great-grandmother.

> Elizabeth Durrant
> Date: Feb. 18, 1932
> Charge to L. J. Durrant, Provo
> Cost:
> $215.00 vault and coffin
>   31.75 clothes
>   10.00 flowers

12.75 opening grave
$269.50 total

As we searched for Durrants we saw many other entries. We found this one interesting:

Scraped and cleaned bones of a chinese man: $21.00.
Shipped to China.

"Now we are really getting to the bare bones of genealogy," I told Noel. He didn't answer, but he did stare at me for a moment.

Warren Anderson was quite excited when we told him what we were doing. He started telling us about his people. He said that his great-grandfather started out in American Fork as a cabinetmaker and had started making coffins. We told him he ought to write it all down. He declared, "You bet I will."

Our search went on. The city library was our next stop, where we wanted to see the old newspapers. The librarian said they were in a locked room down in the basement. She didn't seem too anxious to let us go inside, but a little of Noel's charm and his sincere request soon brought us the key.

The papers were fascinating, but they were not organized so that we could find much. Just looking made us see so many interesting items about American Fork and its past. We might have stayed all the rest of the day had not Stewart proposed, "Let's go get a hamburger and a milkshake." As interesting as it is to search for one's heritage, the thought of food can, at least at mealtime, lead you to forget the past and live in the present.

After a delicious dinner, we rode around American Fork as Stewart pointed out the homes where the Durrant ancestors had once lived. Noel took pictures of each of them. Some of the homes had been torn down and duplex apartments stood in their place.

By now we were a bit weary but far from bored. Noel suggested, "Let's head for Provo and visit the county courthouse."

As we motored the fifteen miles to Provo, I asked, "What are we going to do at the county courthouse?"

"First we'll go to the recorder's office and look at all the land records. That will tell us when and how your people got their land in American Fork and where it was located. The tax lists are usually there also. These lists will tell us the exact years your people were in certain places."

"How will we find all these things?" I wondered.

"Don't worry, you've got me."

"Yes, but what would I do if you weren't with me?"

"The county people would help you. Sometimes they will let you go right in among the actual records. Other times they will find certain records for you. All this is free unless you want a copy."

"Could I write for these things?"

"Sure you could. Just tell them what you want and give them all the details you already have. They'll look it up for you if your request is reasonable."

"Is the recorder's office the only place we'll visit at the courthouse?" I asked.

"Oh, no, we'll also go to the county clerk's office."

"What will we do there?"

"We'll look at the marriage licenses for your ancestors. We'll also look at the birth and death records. The census records might be there and we'll see what they say about your people. We'll also examine some of the probate records."

"What are those?"

"Those are wills and documents showing what happened to the family estate after certain of your ancestors died. They could also show you inventories of what the family owned."

"How will we find all of this?"

"We'll just ask. They have the probate records indexed. They'll find the packet or file that has all the original papers inside, receipts of debts paid, bills for doctors, and coffin expenses. The packet will also include a list of the heirs."

"Noel, I never dreamed all these records existed."

"That's not all. They might also have military records which would include some of your ancestors. These records would reveal your ancestors' birth dates, their parents' names, places where they've served, and the ranks they held.

"There are also naturalization records for those who became citizens, and there could be voting records. These sometimes give good physical descriptions such as eye and hair color and the height and weight of an individual."

I was amazed. "Noel, how come you know so much about county courthouses?"

"George, in my day I have been in over four hundred courthouses."

"Four hundred!" I was in awe.

"Four hundred," he repeated. "And I've never been in one yet where the people weren't friendly and willing to help."

We still had several miles to go before reaching Provo. Suddenly Noel broke out laughing. "What are you laughing at?" I wanted to know.

"Talking about the courthouses I've visited made me think about something funny that happened to me a few years ago back in Kentucky. I was in the Butler County Courthouse looking for the marriage of one of my ancestors when I ran across a record that indicated that on the fourteenth of October, 1895, a Mr. C. W. Arnold applied for a marriage license so he could marry Monita Belle Lee. But the marriage certificate was never completed. I turned the incomplete license over and saw some writing on the back. I copied down what it said; it's here in my notebook." He read the following:

> The god of love performs in mysterious ways. Blessed are they upon whom he smiles. The sorrows produced by his frowns have made subjects for the insane asylum, made hermits and furnished suicides. Beware of cupid's darts.   —W. S. Holmes, D.C.

> While Arnold was dreaming sweet dreams of connubial bliss Marion Haws stole away the idol of his heart. So he awoke from his dream of bliss to realize that it was only a dream!! The records of this office show the caprice of woman.   —W. S. Holmes, D.C.

I chuckled at Noel's story. I envied him for all his visits to all those courthouses.

Noel continued his story. "I kept looking at the records there and I found out that Monita Belle Lee and Marion Haws were married on the thirtieth of October, just sixteen days after she broke old C. W.'s heart. But C. W. didn't give up, and the records show that he married Miss M. C. Cartwright just two months later."

"I'm glad old C. W. made it," I responded, feeling that somehow I now knew him. "The old records sure can bring people back to life."

"They sure can," Noel agreed, as we pulled into a parking spot near the courthouse.

Once inside the beautiful marbled halls of the court-house, Stewart and I followed close behind our great guide. He walked along with the confidence that comes to those who have been in over four hundred such places.

Our first stop was the county clerk's office. "She sure is a pretty county clerk," I whispered to Noel, as a girl walked to the counter.

"Can I help you?" she asked.

"She's not *the* clerk, she's *a* clerk," Noel corrected. Then he turned to the girl. "Yes, we would like to look for the marriage license of Willard Albert Durrant and Marinda Mayne."

The girl quickly returned with a microfilm. She inserted it in the machine, turned the film forward, and there it was. What a thrill it was to read:

> Utah County Marriage License
> Bert Durrant of American Fork and Marinda Mayne
> of Alpine
> 23 yrs. old, 21 yrs. old
> Lic. 12 March 1912
> Married same day at Provo
> By J. E. Booth, Judge 4th Judicial District Court
> Signed: Marinda Mayne and Bert Durrant
> Witnesses: Margaret Bean, Vilate Knudsen

We then asked for and received the copy of my grand-parents' marriage license.

>William A. Durrant   Both of American Fork
>Eliza Conder   Both 17 years old
>Father of Wm., Mother of Eliza gave consent for
>   marriage
>License 7 June 1888
>Married same day in American Fork
>By Wm. M. Bromley Bishop of A.F. Ward
>Witnesses: John Durrant, Sarah Conder

I ordered paper copies of these entries and for three dollars I now owned these prized possessions.

We found much information in the recorder's office about Durrant land, but time ran out. The office would soon be closed.

As we drove away, I felt that I was a man of experience. If I visited just 399 more courthouses I would be as confident as Noel is at this work.

As we drove back toward American Fork I realized that our day was nearly over. "Noel, we aren't going to get it all done today, are we?"

"No," he replied. "We'll never really get done, but if we do a little at a time we'll be able to get a clear picture of your people."

We just had time to do one more activity before we had to head home: to visit some older folks who had known my grandparents.

As we approached their home, I hesitated. "Noel, are you sure they'll want us to bother them about something like this?"

His look was discerning.

"Oh sure, they'll love to tell you all they know. On my recent trip to Kentucky, I was told about a ninety-year-old Negro lady who was living in a rest home. I went to visit her. I had some old pictures and I asked her to tell me about them. She recognized the people and started to talk. I turned on the tape recorder and just listened. Her memory was excellent, and she could recall a good amount about my second great-grandfather, Alexander Hunt. She knew him personally. She told me that his wife, my second great-grandmother, was a clean, well-dressed lady who loved beautiful things and always had a flower garden. She also told me that this woman was a very intelligent person. This elderly lady gave me very precious information."

As we walked toward the house, I asked, "Well, should we ask these people questions or what?"

"We'll ask them about a few things to get them going, but sometimes if we ask too many questions we cut them off. Just get them started and let them talk. They'll come up with some gems. Show them the pictures you have; that will prompt them."

Sure enough, Noel was right. These good people, Delbert and Ora Chipman, told us all they could remember about my grandparents. Every word that they related was a priceless pearl that until now had lain hidden under the surface of the past.

Visiting people such as Delbert and Ora was another of Noel's many excellent suggestions. He is indeed a masterful heritage hunter.

As the sun was now sinking over the western mountains, we said good-bye to Stewart. Noel and I then drove the fifty miles back to Noel's home in Farmington. There was not a moment's silence as we rode along, and every word was about the past and those wonderful people whose reflections were becoming clearer and clearer. I felt good as I thought, *I shall see them again someday, and when I do they won't be strangers.*

I took Noel home. Then as I drove back down the highway, I almost shouted out, "How could I forget! I was going to ask Noel how Christopher Layton could be his double ancestor!" I had been so interested in my ancestors that I forgot. Oh well, there would be other chances to find out.

4   *Getting on the Case*

S everal days had passed since my visit to my hometown. I was eager to do more heritage hunting. I didn't know what to do next, and so I went to Noel's office. I knocked and heard a loud, "Come in."

Noel didn't look up as I entered. On his desk was a huge pile of papers and several boxes of microfilm. While searching frantically through the material, Noel seemed most distressed. I had never seen him like this. I meekly asked, "Noel, what's wrong?"

Still throwing papers and moving his little boxes, he answered with words I shall never forget. "George, I have lost my senses!"

You can imagine my alarm. How could I ever learn about my people if my great detective had lost his senses. I paused for a few seconds and watched him, and then I decided to find a phone and call a psychiatrist.

Just as I turned to leave, I heard his gleeful shout. "I've found my census!" I walked closer to his desk and in his hand I could see a box containing a microfilm of part of the 1850 census.

Noel had found his census, but I felt I would soon lose mine if we couldn't get back to American Fork and continue my family search. "When can we go back?" I pleaded.

Noel quickly replied, "My work here is too pressing; I can't go again for a month."

"I can't wait that long before I work on this project again." There was depression in my tone.

Sensing that I needed encouragement, Noel assured me. "George you don't have to go to American Fork every time you want to find clues about the past. But you're lucky you grew up in American Fork."

"Yes, I know that," I quickly agreed. "It sure beats Lehi, Pleasant Grove and all those other towns."

"What I mean is that American Fork is nearby. It is easy for you to go home. Think of those people who can't go back to their old hometowns because they are too far away."

I felt sorry for such people and suggested, "Couldn't they at least go there during their vacation?"

Noel smiled. "Ah, yes, they sure could, and they would never have a finer vacation than going home for the purpose of doing those things that would help them learn of their heritage."

I was proud that my answer had pleased my great teacher. Then his face took on a look of pity. "Some folks can't even do that because money or distance forbids it."

In a sorrowful tone I added, "I guess those people won't be able to do anything to learn of their past."

Noel was hopeful. "Sure they can. They can't go home in a car, a train or a plane, but they can take the best of all vehicles home. They can get into their memory and drive home in a second."

"Hey, with the price of gasoline, that might be the best way to go," I pointed out.

Noel stood up. "Speaking of going, I've got to go. I've found some new photographs of some of Christopher Layton's children and I'm getting them enlarged so that I can include them in the book."

"Don't leave yet," I begged. "What can I do to learn more about my people?"

Noel walked toward the door. "Get into your memory and go home. When you are there, write down what you see and hear and smell and, most of all, what you feel."

I was getting the vision. I walked with Noel for a block or so to seek further help. He suggested that I start a search of my present residence from basement to attic, looking for anything that would offer clues to my past. "What could I find?" I asked.

"Perhaps there will be old letters to or from your parents. There could be photographs of you when you were young and maybe even some photographs of your ancestors. You'll find your old school report cards, school yearbooks, and certificates of various kinds. Your own home is like a mine filled with golden nuggets of the past. Go home and get out your pick and shovel and start mining."

With these words, Noel hastened his pace and moved away from me. I stopped, and as he was about out of voice range I shouted, "Anything else?"

He called back, "Yes, write a letter to each of your brothers and sisters. Explain to them what you're doing. Ask them to send you copies of things that they think would help, and, if you can afford it, call them on the phone and talk with them about the good old days."

Noel was gone and so was my lunch hour. I thought to myself, *There is no time now for genealogy. I will get at it tonight, but tonight I have a meeting. I will do it tomorrow night; no, that's my son's basketball game. Saturday I will have all day—after I get the garden planted, clean out the garage, and take the children on a promised picnic."*

Suddenly, I heard in my mind the words of my sister-in-law. "Write a personal history? I don't even have time to live one!"

Noel had given me so many great ideas, and now there didn't seem to be time to do them. Discouraged, I hung my head and walked back to work. There was some hope because I would be retiring in just twenty-three more years. Perhaps there would be time then for pedigrees and histories.

I must confess that this book almost ended at this point. It seems as though so many of life's really valuable ventures crash and sink on the rocky and jagged shore of a too-busy life. *Besides, I thought, who would ever care about my history or my pedigree? Nothing exciting ever happened to me or any of my ancestors. After all, I never have been very important. I wasn't all-state; I wasn't student body president. I was just a private, not an officer, while I served in the peacetime army. I haven't achieved any great honors, and my ancestors were really common folk. So who cares if I never do any genealogy?*

Through this kind of thinking, I had just about come to a state of that too-expensive peace that finally comes when you talk yourself out of something that could be so very worthwhile.

Just before I went under, drowning in the sea of excuses, I grabbed hold of the liferaft of desire and softly said, "There *is* someone who cares about my history and my people, and that person is me." I knew that I couldn't make it with a single mighty surge, but if I took this ancestral search a stroke at a time I could make it.

After all, there would be some extra time each day and once in awhile a whole half-day. I remembered Noel's words: "We will never really get done, but if we do a little at a time we will be able to get a clear picture of your people."

That night I called Noel on the phone. "It's me," I said.

"That's what I was afraid of."

"Hey, Noel, I've decided there aren't any deadlines on my genealogy."

"You mean all your ancestors are still alive?" He was astonished.

"No, I don't mean that. I mean I don't have to have it all done by this weekend or even by the first of the year."

I could tell that Noel was proud of me, and he added, "Yes, this work, or, I should say, this pleasure of seeking our family heritage, takes a long time. When you embark on something this large, you must approach it in a most organized manner."

When he said the word *organized* a cold chill went up and down my spine. If he had said, "You need to be handsome to do this work," I could have qualified. If it took great intelligence, I would qualify. If creative talent was required, again I would qualify. Humility—I could muster that. But to be organized—that was asking too much.

Noel's voice broke the silence. "Hello, hello, are you there?"

I finally spoke. "Noel, I really need your help. How do I get organized?"

Noel talked fast. "Get a box or a file cabinet. Buy some manila folders. Label three folders with these headings: childhood, youth, and adult.

Then label seven other folders with these headings: parents, grandparent, grandparent, great-grandparent, great-grandparent, great-grandparent, great-grandparent, and include the names and years of birth and death for each."

Noel was truly a genius at organization. "Where do I get the folders?" I wanted to know. Before he could answer, I asked, "What kind of a box? Could it be an orange crate or what?"

Noel was also wise. "George you figure those things out for yourself; that's the way you'll grow." I heard the phone click, and I knew that Noel, the detective, was gone.

"Marilyn," I shouted to my wife, "I need a box. Have we got any kind of a box?"

"How big?" she asked.

"The size folders would fit into."

"What kind of folders?"

"Vanilla ones," I instructed.

"Vanilla?" she asked in a startled tone. "You mean manila, don't you?"

"Whatever."

Soon she had a fine box in her hand. When I saw her with this box, I knew that she would be a perfect genealogical partner. After all, if I had to search the house for clues to the past, I would have to have her do it. For it had been seven years since I had ever found anything on my own, successfully, while searching in the house. When I used to search for hours, she would always say, "Here it is, right where I told you it was." It's sort of a sixth sense with her.

I spoke to her softly. "Marilyn, I'll pay you most generously if you'll be of assistance to me in helping me find my history and establish my pedigree."

These tender, poetic words seemed to reach deep into her heart as she replied, "I'd much sooner just watch TV."

However, I knew she would help me find my ancestors because she often wonders how I came to be.

I was now committed to the work of discovering my heritage. I had the time, a little now and a little then, and as much as four hours on some days. I was organized, for I would soon have my box with its labeled but empty files. I had a research assistant who was living right there in my home, and somewhere in the house were hidden many clues to the past. With all these things in my mind, I was pleasantly surprised when Marilyn asked me if I wanted some ice cream. "Yes, please, and make it manila."

The next morning before I left for work, I asked my wife a favor. "Marilyn, today in between fixing the meals, taking the children here and there, planting the petunias, going to the store, and attending your calligraphy class, could you look for old pictures and old letters and other old stuff?"

Her "you've got to be kidding" look assured me that she'd do it.

Sure enough, that night the card table was piled high with scrapbooks, certificates, letters, pictures, and even a blue ribbon with the inscription: "First place in Volleyball, Alpine Days, 1949." I pinned the ribbon to my shirt and began to examine the pile of genealogical gold.

I only had half an hour before I had to be at a meeting, but I knew that would be long enough. I could drop all this material in files in just a few moments. But something went wrong. I couldn't just pick things up and file them. I began to read each paper and to savor every picture. I couldn't go fast. This was better than a TV show or even a sports event.

"Hey, here I am in kilts while I was in Scotland. That day I found out what the Scots wear under their kilts." I was remembering almost every detail of our trip to Scotland. In my mind I could see Loch Lomond. I put that picture aside and picked up another. I smiled as I thought, *There I am, just out of basic training. There is no stripe on my arm. I suppose that was just before they discovered my exceptional ability and promoted me to private first class.* My mind was now filled with my army experiences. I began to feel an urge to write all these thoughts and memories down.

I wondered: *Where are my discharge papers? Oh, here they are. What date did I get out? The army was quite an experience. Here is a pile of letters I wrote to Marilyn while I was in the army. I would love to read them again. Look at this picture. I was a cute little kid. I must have been about two years old here.*

There's Dad in his overalls — he always wore those. I think that's why he didn't go to church. Overalls didn't seem like the proper dress there.

Here we are on our camping trip. We only had four children then.

Oh, no, it is time to go to a meeting! "Marilyn, I will leave this stuff here and file it later. It is taking me longer to go through it than I thought it would."

The next day I saw Noel in the cafeteria. Since he had just finished his lunch, I knew that he was now a full brother and because of that he would be in a mood to help me.

"Noel, I've got a problem."

"Yes, I know you have, George."

"I don't have enough time. Last night I was going to do some work, but I didn't get anywhere." I then explained to him what I had done.

He looked stern. "George, you've got to be strong. Go home and file those things in the file. No matter how interested you are, you must look and file rather than look, read, think, and file. Then when you've got things filed in the childhood, youth, and adult files, you'll be able to go back to the childhood one and, with a pen in hand, write down those things that happened to you as a child.

"Must it be that way?" I asked despondently. "Can't I let my mind wander like an American motor car and just be a Rambler?"

He struck the table. "No!" The conversation ended. I was going to ask him how Christopher Layton could be his double ancestor, but he was in no mood for such a question.

That night Marilyn had found even more material. She took me to an old trunk and we went through all the things there. I didn't have much time, but after following Noel's firm instruction I filed almost everything.

There were several items in each file. The file which I had labeled "parents" was quite full. I wondered what Noel would say if I made a file for each parent instead of putting everything in one file. Thinking that he would approve, I did it.

It was time now for my son's ball game, and I had to leave. But I felt satisfied because so many things were filed. I was truly becoming a genealogical wizard.

As I rode to the game, my mind was still on my records. I was planning ahead. Saturday I would get up early and be a child again. On that day I would relive and write down my wonderful memories of when I was a little kid on the Bert Durrant chicken farm from 1931 to 1941.

Soon the weekend arrived. The Saturday sun was not yet up, but George, Bert and Marinda's ninth child, was up. With plenty of paper and a trusty ball-point pen, I was ready to step back into the past.

I spread all my childhood pictures out before me. My mind hesitated for a time in the present, but then it went speedily into the past—back to ages ten, nine, eight, seven, six, and five. It was hard to go back any further, but there were a few flashes from ages four and even three.

Let's see, age three, that would be about 1935. Who was the president of the country then? What was the price of penny candy? I couldn't remember those things, but I could just barely remember me.

I could remember sitting on my mother's lap. I could remember the old round table at which we sat to eat. I could remember the chickens. But these impressions were hard to write as experiences. My paper was still blank.

I jumped ahead a little. Kindergarten—I would write my memories of kindergarten. Let's see, I started school in September, 1936, but I started kindergarten the year before that.

That means that I started kindergarten at age four. Age four? No wonder I cried and wouldn't stay. I never realized before that I entered kindergarten at age four. That was why I held onto my mother's skirt and cried until she and the teacher agreed that there was no hope that I would remain.

I could remember the great emotional victory it was for me when I started back home with my mother instead of staying in the schoolroom with all those strangers.

I smiled as I considered how my older brother had, through the years, teased me by saying that I was such a baby that I would not go to kindergarten. Now with this new-found evidence, I could fight back. After all, I was only four years old. If I had been five I would have stayed. Already, reconstructing my personal childhood history was paying off with the insights of self-understanding.

After writing about this exciting victory of my young life, I was off and running.

I made no attempt to break the trend of thought by looking for specific dates or names. I wrote as fast as my pen would fly. Because of the speed, my handwriting wasn't very legible. Actually, it isn't too good even if I write slowly; but I could get it typed later.

As I wrote on and on, I realized that I must be a little careful so that my experiences and feelings could at least be read.

I wrote many things that morning. I couldn't include everything that I wrote, but the next chapter will provide a bit of the flavor of what I wrote that day about my childhood, as well as what I have written since.

5   *Evidence Along the Way*

I was a baby when I was born, and to my mother for as long as she lived I always remained her baby. Because of that she spoiled me. My seven older brothers and sisters would point out to her, "You are spoiling him."

I remember thinking, *Mind your own business because I am enjoying it.*

She couldn't spoil me with *things* because we didn't really have much money. She just spoiled me with love, and that love did more to shape my life than all the schools I ever attended, all the friends I ever had, and all the books I've ever read.

Kindergarten presented the first great crisis in my life and is my first vivid memory. My mother, having seen me safely there, tried to leave me. I sensed she was going and began to scream. The teacher pulled me back, but I caught my mother's skirt and would not let go. After several torturous moments, I won the victory.

Mother took me home, and I had another glorious year at her side. I often wonder how great I could have been had I gone to kindergarten. My mind might have been keener but my heart could (or is it would?) have been different. I've always lived more from my heart than from my head, and so perhaps the extra year at home was for the best.

I was a cute little child; at least mom always told everyone that I was. However, I was sort of a slow learner. My first-grade teacher held up two fully colored books titled *Snow White*. She said, "We are going to have a contest. The boy and girl in the class who does the best for the next month will each receive one of these books."

I've never tried so hard. I will always remember when my best friend was awarded the book a month later. That was my first really big disappointment. It was not the last, for I had many disappointments along the way. Mom kept telling me that I was a most special boy, and somehow that balanced the disappointments.

Have you ever heard the cooing of a mourning dove? I remember hearing that sound during my childhood days as I walked home from school. My journey led me north on First East until I came to the south end of the mill lane. In this picturesque setting a stream ran along the side of the old, winding dirt road. Trees arched over from each side of the road and touched. It was while I walked through this heavenly place that I often heard the sound of the mourning doves.

I am not sure if I was a happy child or not, but when I would hear that indescribably moody song I would feel like saying, "Those sounds and me are one and the same."

Even now when I hear the cooing of a dove, I find myself again as a small child walking up the old mill lane looking in the stream for a small trout that was always there. So I suppose that as a child I was as happy or as sad as is the song of the dove.

In the summer when there were no school cares I would take off my shoes and go barefoot. I would roam the fields and the creek-bed forests that were to the north and east of our place. As I ran across the green grass of the city pasture, I would often hear the sound of a meadowlark. When I was up there in that paradise I had feelings in my heart that I can't capture in words. But as best as I can remember, I felt just like the sound of a meadowlark.

So, I can sum up my childhood by declaring that my emotions, my feelings, and my thoughts were like the cooing of a dove or the song of a meadowlark or somewhere in between.

My boyhood soon faded, and the confusing years of youth came crashing toward me. My schoolwork was better now — my grades had risen to C's. Now there were new pressures. I wanted to be big, and I was small. I wanted to be the best athlete, and I was at best average. I wanted to be popular and I was, but only with a few.

My father was an honest man who worked hard and expected me to do the same. We raised chickens. I gathered eggs and cleaned out coops, and I hated every minute of it. However, I did it willingly because I had to. My mother taught me to love life, and my father taught me to work. Now I know that neither is possible without the other.

These were difficult years because I felt a personal insignificance. Again, in these times, my mother came to the rescue.

I would come home from a school day having achieved no great victories in the classroom, in the gymnasium, or in the social circles. Mom would greet me. She was always there when I came home from the war — I mean from school.

"Do you want a peanut butter sandwich?" she would ask.

My brothers, hearing her, would comment: "Let him make it himself. What's the matter with him? Has he got a broken arm?"

I wouldn't answer until they were gone. "Mom, the reason I like you to make sandwiches for me is because when you make them they taste better." She would smile and I would know that I would have sandwiches forever. Yes, she treated me in a most special, kind, and generous way; and in return I tried to do the same to her.

I would sit on her lap, and she would run her fingers through my hair and say, "George, you are special." I wondered why my coach, or the girls, or the teachers didn't know what mother knew. I even wondered why I didn't know, but somehow I did know because she told me.

On to college — almost failing grades were my trademark. I talked to mom. "I'm quitting school."

"Don't quit school."

"I'm quitting. I'm not doing any good there."

"Don't quit," she begged.

"Why not?"

"Because what you are going to be in life you've got to go to school to be."

"What am I going to be?"

"I have no idea, but you've got to go to school to be it."

"I'm quitting."

She cried.

"I was just kidding," I responded. And so I continued. I still wonder after all these years what I'm going to be.

My life would have been so different if it hadn't been for the love and encouragement of my mother and the firm, silent leadership of my father.

In the army I began my career as a private, but after only two years of dedicated service I had risen through the ranks all the way to private first class. This showed me what a talented man can really do.

I found a girl, Marilyn Burnham, and after getting to know her I decided she deserved the very best. So I asked her to marry me. She agreed, and I gave her a ring.

Her mother later pointed out, "At least our daughter isn't marrying a spendthrift."

Her father added, "You don't often see a diamond like that; the light has to be just right."

We had little money, but we made it.

Eight children came and blessed our lives. Our oldest son was born while we were in the army. He cost us eight dollars. I often looked at him as he grew up and exclaimed, "You cost us eight dollars, but as far as I am concerned you have been worth every cent of it."

He countered, "Gee, dad, I sure do appreciate your saying that."

Through the years, I have been highly blessed by the Lord. On many occasions I have felt his hand and have been guided by his influence.

Once as I prepared to go to Korea with the army, I was greatly depressed with the thought of leaving my wife and young son. The tears of my wife dampened my pillow each night, and I prayed nearly a million prayers that I would not have to go.

At that same time our baby son needed an operation, but I could not remain to be with him. I flew to Fort Lewis. While there, I waited several days for a ship. During that depressing week I received a letter which said:

> I took our little son to the hospital for his operation but the doctor examined him and said there was no longer a problem.
>
> I suppose the prayer you said as you held him in your arms the night before you left has brought about a miracle.

Tears filled my eyes as I looked toward heaven and almost heard the Lord say, "This is the answer to your prayers. Go to Korea, and while you are gone I will take care of your family." What a blessing! What comfort! What joy!

I wrote all morning. Noon came in what seemed like moments rather than hours. It was time to go back to my present world. There were things to do with the family. I wanted to help them have memories as pleasant as my own. I wanted them to feel as good about their childhood as I did about mine.

That afternoon was a happy one for me. As I thought back, I was amazed that I could recall so much. That which I remembered gave me a much clearer picture of myself and a greater understanding of why I am me.

I could hardly wait to show Noel what I had done. The following week, I went to his office. His door was open, and I entered without knocking. I placed the pages on his desk and said, "Read this."

Without looking up he picked up the papers and gazed at them. "I would like to. What language are they written in?"

"You've got them upside down," I explained.

"Oh, yes, I've had some paleography courses so I will be able to decipher them.

I wondered if paleography meant having the same man for both a great-great-grandfather and great-grandfather, but I didn't ask. I departed quickly so that he could read my masterpiece.

Noel approached me at lunch. "It's great, George." My heart pounded. My hero, my teacher had liked what I had done. He asked me how I had gone about my task. I told him, and he explained to me some things he felt one should do in writing a personal history.

"You, the author, should be as accurate as possible. To do this you'll need to be truthful and not try to gloss things up. You don't need to make yourself out as a saint. You can make a positive point out of a negative event. You should try to motivate people to do good.

"In your writing you can explain what makes you tick as a human being. Build in solutions to problems you have faced. Discuss your personality and feelings. Describe the influences in your life that made you feel certain ways and do certain things.

"Help people to actually know you. Folklore can be included, but don't claim it as fact. You can add, 'This is what I feel happened.'

"You can write chronologically from birth to death. In the middle you can cover your life by subjects. Some subjects may overlap others chronologically, but you can back up after completing one subject and cover another."

I was grateful for this help because there were many parts of my life that I still desired to write about.

I had learned that thinking back on your past life and writing your experiences was an inspiring project.

My memories made me feel grateful.

God had indeed treated me as if I were special.

6 *The Nearest Witnesses*

During the next several weeks I remembered and wrote many experiences from my past. I could have done more if it had not been for picnics, camping trips, weeds in the garden, softball games, work, and laziness.

Noel checked on my progress from time to time. He would make me jealous by declaring, "Look what I've done." He would then tell me some extremely fascinating things he had discovered about his ancestors.

I remember the day he returned from his trip to Kentucky and showed me a picture. As I was gazing at the stern-looking horseman, Noel related this story.

"Dr. Alex Hunt, my great-great-grandfather, was a well-known man in the Mud River country of Kentucky. He would ride over the hills and ford the streams on his old white horse named Duke to get to his many patients. Duke was born in the bluegrass part of the state and somehow got over to the western part. My Great-great-grandfather Hunt bought the horse, and for the next twenty-five years Duke carried the doctor over Butler and Muhlenburg counties on his calls. Every day Dr. Hunt would cross the Mud River on the little ferry which he owned. As the boat crossed the river he would stand and hold Duke's bridle.

"Every time they crossed, Duke reached over and took a good long swig of the fresh river water. One morning while Duke was getting his drink the ferry bumped something. Duke lost his balance and fell headfirst right into the cold water—saddle and all. He came up swimming, and Dr. Hunt made a grab for the saddle bags that contained his stock of medicine. I have been told that my great-great-grandfather was cussing mad. He led old Duke up the hill and unsaddled him and tried to dry out the saddle. The funny part is that old Duke was as mad as the doctor." Noel pointed to the picture while he explained. "This picture shows how old Duke expressed his anger. See how his ears are back?"

"You mean your great-great-grandfather's ears?" I asked.

"No, I mean Duke's," Noel replied disgustedly.

I looked at the picture a little longer. "Noel, you've got all the interesting ancestors. You've got Christopher Layton twice and Dr. Hunt and old Duke." Noel's ears sort of went back and he looked as if he were about to hit me, but before he could I continued. "If my ancestors were as interesting as yours I would be as good at genealogy as you are."

Noel quickly responded: "How do you know your ancestors aren't as interesting as mine? You don't even know anything about them. No one is interesting until you get to know them."

I immediately felt guilty. It seemed as if Noel was always on my back. I turned and took a step toward the door. "Where are you going?" Noel's voice was like a command.

"I'm going to find out about my ancestors."

"Where are you going to look, and where are you going to start?"

"Well, first I am going to . . . I will probably . . . I don't know."

"George, come and sit down and let's talk. Let's get you organized." I turned around, reentered the office, and sat by Noel's desk.

Dr. Alexander Hunt on his horse Duke

"Look at this," he instructed as he reached in his desk drawer and pulled out a rather large but blank pedigree chart. "Bring your chair over to this side," he beckoned in a patient tone. When I could see the chart he asked, "Where should we start?"

"Let's start with my great-grandfather," I answered. "I've wondered about him ever since we visited the cemetery."

"Great-grandfather?" Noel's tone was almost shocked.

"Sure, that's where you started. You're always telling me about Christopher Layton, and then today you told me about Alexander Hunt. They are your great-grandfathers, so that is where I want to start."

Noel patted me on the shoulder with great compassion. "George, I didn't *start* with my great-grandfathers. I started with me and worked back, generation by generation."

Noel, sensing that he had wounded me a little by his rebuke, now seemed more patient. "Let's start with number one on the pedigree chart. In your case who would that be?"

I thought for a few seconds and timidly offered, "Would that be me?"

Noel smiled broadly. "Good, you are beginning to be a great genealogist." I smiled but still remained humble.

Noel pulled his pen from his pocket and wrote my name on the first line of the simple pedigree chart he had drawn up. As you can see, Noel is a pretty good draftsman as well as being a very good writer:

"Who would be next on the chart?" Noel asked with great patience.

"Well, let's see, I suppose it would be my parents."

"Right," Noel shouted. "You're really hot now. What's your father's name?"

"Bert Durrant." I had pride in the fact that I knew the answer.

"Bert? Was that his full name?"

"Well, that's what everyone called him. But his real name was Willard Albert Durrant."

"Let's write his real name." Noel's pen moved across the paper. "What was your mother's name?"

"Marinda Mayne."

"Did your mother have a middle name?"

"I think so."

"What was it?"

"Well, it was . . . let's see. I guess I'll have to call my brother, Stewart. He would know."

"George, I don't like to be critical, because basically you are a good fellow and I like you. But how can you accuse your ancestors of not being interesting when you don't even know your mother's middle name?" I cringed and hung my head with a degree of shame.

Noel, sensing my dejection, broke the silence. "Don't be discouraged. Our first task is to find your mother's middle name. That will be the beginning, and from there we will find out so much about those two wonderful people that you will be able, if you desire, to write a book about them."

"A book!" I was amazed.

"Sure."

"Well, I'd like to write something."

"You can, George, you can."

My dejection was gone. Dejection always flies away when one accepts a great challenge.

"What do I do first, Noel?"

"You've already got the manila folders for your parents, and in those folders you have a collection of pictures and other papers. Remember, we found their marriage license in the courthouse in Provo, and we found the death information at both the cemetery and the city hall. You have already started, George. You're a great genealogist; you're on your way. You should also talk to your brothers and sisters and other relatives about their memories of your parents. You could also go talk to Delbert Chipman. He seemed to know your father and mother well. Then just sit down and write your own memories of home and the folks."

"Gee, Noel, there's a lot I can do, isn't there?"

"There sure is. There is no limit to this work. You can do as much as your time and energy will allow."

"I'll never get as much done as you have."

"You don't have to. I do this as my professional work and also as my hobby. Just do what you can. Ten pages would be far better than no pages. Besides, if you want people to read what you write, your writing can't be too long. But the better you know your parents, the more selective you can be with what you write about them. You can write down those things that will make your father and mother really live."

I looked at Noel with deep admiration. He really knew how to inspire me. Christopher Layton could sure be proud of his great-grandson, I mean his great-great-grandson.

Talking about mother and father during the next few visits with my brothers and sisters was an unforgettable experience. We talked about father's deep love of the outdoors, his constant search for minerals in the mines of American Fork Canyon. I had often heard that he had been in a mine cave-in, but I had never found out all of the details.

We discussed the chicken ranch where father had made a living after he gave up mining. Yes, we talked and talked of those golden days when dad and mom were alive, and, as we did, I loved each of my brothers and sisters more. There is something so special about having the same parents and the same heritage and so many of the same memories.

Life is good when one considers his family. Of course, there are some memories that are not so sweet. There are struggles economically, religiously, and sometimes we have inner-family strife. These things are often a part of life. We all struggle as we grow up. Strangely enough, from those struggles come the experiences that are most meaningful and character-building.

The more I learned about my parents, the more I came to know myself. Looking back at them made me want even more to be a good father and husband. I began to realize that even if I didn't write down all that I was learning, it didn't matter. Just learning about them made me better understand life's purpose and my direction. However, if I could write them down in an organized way or at least record them on tape, my children and their children could someday catch a glimpse of what I have felt while looking back at my dear mother and father.

You can imagine my joy when my brother Stewart handed me a history that my mother had written about her life. I had known of this priceless document but had somehow overlooked it. I wanted to run to Noel and shout, "Look, Noel, this is my mother's history written in her own handwriting!" The following night I read and read. Tears of joy moistened my eyes as I saw my mother as a child in Alpine, Utah. Then I saw her as a youth. I felt that I was there when she fell in love with my father. Then the children came. Of all the reading I have ever done, nothing was as gripping as my mother's history as she had written it.

As I finished the final page, I stared out the window. God had been so good to me by giving me such a mother. So much of what she felt I now feel. So much that was dear to her is now dear to me. I felt great security as I gently thought, *My mother and I are truly as one.*

A week later Noel asked me, "Well, what's your mother's middle name?"

I quickly answered, "Elizabeth." I didn't even take time to catch a breath before I added, "And she was born in Alpine, Utah." Without letting him break my pace, I told him all about my mother.

He was astonished, and for the first time I imagined that he was a little envious that I had such an interesting ancestor.

"How do you know all of this?" he asked. I then revealed my mother's written history and laid it on the desk in front of him. He examined it for several silent moments. "What a treasure! It is amazing what you can find when you really start to search.

"What about your father?" he asked. "Did he leave a history?"

"No, but I did learn a lot about him." When I got to the part about his being trapped in a mine cave-in, he asked, "When was that?" I told him the date that I had found in mother's writings.

Noel asked me to spend my lunch hour with him. We didn't eat; instead we went to the library. We looked through the microfilms of the old state newspapers. Finally he shouted, "Here it it!" I was amazed. There before my eyes was a copy of the actual newspaper article. He moved away from it and urged, "Go ahead and read it." I read the newspaper account of the cave-in.

(Special to the Telegram) Saturday Evening, July 1, 1911

AMERICAN FORK, July 1 - Timothy Smith and Albert Derrant are breathing free air again and say they feel absolutely no ill effects from their imprisonment for thirty-four and one-half hours in the tunnel of the Whirlwind mine up American Fork canyon.

They were rescued from their tomb last midnight and immediately ate heartily, after which they were brought to their homes here. Both men were on the streets today in the best of spirits. Neither showed the least effect of his uncomfortable experience. Both were cold when removed from the tunnel, but were soon warmed up and talked cheerfully of their past troubles.

The cave-in occurred about 200 feet from the mouth of the tunnel at 1:30 o'clock Thursday afternoon. Back of the cave-in was a space extending 200 feet that was higher and therefore dry. The air was not the best, but the miners say they did not suffer.

When a horse and scraper were brought into use the rescuers made real headway. The mud and slush seemed to pour out like they were coming from a reservoir and the shovels could do little with the waste. The scraper, however, began making headway and then a hole about nine inches in diameter was made in the muddy wall. Rescuers crawled up on this mud heap and reaching in, pulled the two miners through the little opening by their feet.

When I had finished I was choked with emotion and whispered, "I'd love to have a copy of that."

Within a few seconds Noel had the librarian make me a copy. We walked back to Noel's office. As we entered and sat down, I asked, "Did you read my mother's history, Noel?"

"I sure did," replied the heritage hunter. "She's a great lady, but she gets a little confused at times."

"What do you mean?" I asked. "I thought she wrote really well."

"Listen to this." He thumbed through the pages. "Oh, here it is." He read the passage:

The baby was due about the last of October. Bert always went hunting deer about the 19th of October. That year he went as usual. The next day our baby came. But it was not a girl as I had hoped. I am so thankful for the fact that it was a boy as he has been a wonderful son. Afton was so disappointed she cried and said that Heavenly Father did not answer prayers, but when she saw the baby he was so cute with lots of black hair she said, "Wouldn't he have made a cute girl?"

"If your mother thought you were cute she must have been confused." I was a little shocked at Noel's remark. I quickly pulled my comb from my pocket and ran it through my nearly-black hair.

I spoke firmly. "It seems to me that it is you who is confused, Noel. I couldn't look like I do now unless I had been a really beautiful baby."

Noel smiled, but he didn't laugh. "There's a lot of your mother in you."

"Why do you say that?"

"Well, she liked the same two birds which you mentioned."

"What birds? How do you know that she liked birds?"

"It's right here; I'll read it":

> I did not like our house out in the fields in the winter, but it was beautiful in the summer, and the birds used to sing all the time. I especially liked the meadowlarks and the mourning doves, and we used to love to hunt wild flowers. We always hunted wild flowers for Decoration Day as there were not many other flowers around at that time.

Noel commented, "Those are the same two birds, meadowlarks and mourning doves, that you mentioned in your account of your childhood days."

Somehow Noel's observation caused my soul to tingle. I hoped with all my heart that I could be like my mother.

"I thought you told me you were your mother's favorite," Noel recalled.

"Well, I was, sort of. At least she treated me as if I were, but she treated us all that way. I was the baby and I think she liked me the best."

"No, she didn't. In her history she speaks more lovingly of another family member."

"Who?" I asked eagerly.

"Listen." Noel read as I skeptically waited:

> I also milked the cow. I did not think the boys got all the milk and they did not like to milk, and as we needed all the milk we could get, I milked most of the time. We had some nice cows who gave a lot of milk, and I used to churn butter about twice a week. We had one cow I will never forget. We raised her from a tiny calf. She was a twin and as black as coal. When she was born we did not think she would live, but she did, she became a regular pet.

She would follow me around and I would talk to her. She seemed to understand what I said. When she became a cow she gave such a lot of rich milk. I used to wonder how such a little cow could give so much. I always milked her and I could milk her in the pasture or any place and she would never move. At a certain time she seemed to know it was time to be milked. I would sing "How Firm a Foundation" to her and when I was through singing all five verses, I was through milking.

She got into the peach tree one night when there were frozen peaches on the ground and ate a lot of them. The next morning she died. I cried and said I never wanted another cow. We later bought another one, but I never sang to her.

When he finished reading, Noel looked me directly in the eyes. "Did your mother ever sing 'How Firm a Foundation' to you?"

"Not that I can remember," I timidly replied.

"That's because she loved the cow more."

I quickly changed the subject. "You know, Noel, reading my mother's story made me feel I was right there with her as she grew up. I cried a little when I read about my mother's great sadness. Let me take the history. Let's see, it's right here." I read:

When I was eleven years old a very sad thing happened in our family. My dear mother gave birth to a beautiful little baby girl who was born dead. My mother was very sick and she almost died.

She had a severe emotional breakdown after the birth of her baby, and she never was the same. She was very melancholy and she also had spells when she was very irrational. In August my father had to take her to the State Mental Hospital. It breaks my heart to write about it as we needed her so much. My little brother was only two years old, but we did the best we could.

My sister Maggie stayed home for awhile but she went back to work and Celestia also went to American Fork to work the next winter. So I was left home to take care of my little brother, my father, and Joseph who was ten years old.

My father was so very kind and good to me or I do not believe I could have done as I did after my mother was taken away. He was always there to help me when he could. Little Stephen was like his shadow and father always wanted to take him with him wherever he went. Stephen would gather up rocks and play with them and other things as long as he could see my father or me around. My father was very quiet after mother was gone and the only time he smiled was when he talked to Stephen or to Joe or me.

"My mother was a great woman, Noel, and I think it was because she knew sorrow that she came to be the quality lady that she was. Listen to this happy, sad moment of her life that occurred when she left home to marry my father."

On the 11th of March my father took me down to Maggie's in the wagon as he had to go to American Fork anyway. Steve went with us. I was very unhappy when I left home for the last time as I hated to leave my father who had always been so good to me. And I hated to leave Steve as he and I were so close. I had been the only mother he had known, and although he was twelve years old, I felt he still needed me, and so did he. Tears were in my father's eyes as he kissed me good-bye, and I was almost tempted to go back home with him.

"Somehow, Noel, it's stories like that which I treasure. You know, little things somehow mean so very much."

"That's right." I had never heard Noel sound more serious. "That's why when we write our histories we need to tell how we felt about what happened rather than just tell what happened."

"Noel, I've got to go. But first, should I just tell you something?"

"Sure, go ahead."

"Noel, I love my mother with all my heart, and just thinking about her makes me want to be everything she ever dreamed I would be. As I related in my history, she used to hold me on her lap and run her fingers through my hair and tell me that I was special. I feel special because anyone with a mother like her had to be special. Thanks for listening, Noel, and thanks for letting me share her history with you. She would have been proud to know that you read about her life and that you understood."

Noel and I shook hands. Because he had a mother, he understood; and because of our love for our mothers, we shared a great love for each other. I feel that God's greatest plan was to give us each a mother.

As I walked away, Noel called out, "Forget my comment about the cow. I only uttered it to see if I could milk a little humility out of you." I walked on, pretending not to hear, but I felt like a cow walking in tall grass, utterly tickled!

I could tell so many things which I learned about my parents, but let me conclude by just telling what I personally remember about them.

One day in Nashville, Tennessee, while my wife and children and I were at an amusement park called Opryland, I had a dream about the past. We had ridden many rides and had eaten everything from cotton candy to Swedish waffles. The sun had just gone down and, being a bit weary, I found a seat in a little outdoor theater. Some country-western singers were providing entertainment on the stage.

I was in a most reflective mood as I listened to their words and music. They began to sing a song which I had never heard before. I remember the words: "Country road, take me home."

Those words caused a dream to begin to unfold in my heart.

In my mind I could see the country road that had so often taken me home. It was the old Alpine Road which turns north

Marinda Mayne Durrant (standing next to banner) at graduation from eighth grade

from downtown American Fork and continues on for about five miles to Alpine.

In my mind I walked that old road again as I had done so many times as a child. Finally, after a one-mile hike, I spied my childhood home. The house was surrounded by a spacious green lawn, and surrounding the lawn was a white wood and wire fence. In the front yard by the mailbox was a row of locust trees which towered high into the clear blue sky and cast a cool shade across most of the lawn. I passed the mailbox and walked under the giant cedar trees that grew on each side of the sidewalk leading to the cement porch.

I sniffed the lilacs and climbed the three stairs up to the porch. Looking to my right, I could see into the big bay window that was in the corner of our large kitchen.

My heart almost leaped within me as I saw my father looking out at me through the window while he sat in his rocking chair. He was dressed in his bibbed overalls. His hair was lightened somewhat by the grey hair that grew amidst the more prominent dark hair of his youth.

I opened the door and entered. My mother was standing by the pots and pans that covered the hot end of our old coal range. She smiled and greeted me, but continued with her cooking.

All seven of my brothers and sisters were home. Soon we all gathered at the round table that was in the center of the big kitchen.

Mother placed her delicious cooking before us, and after a prayer we ate. With her grey hair combed straight back into a bun, my mother was up and down many times as she served us one of those unforgettable meals.

It was so good to be back home again and so good to see my father and my mother.

Suddenly someone shouted, "Daddy!" and I was no longer in the home of my childhood. I was back in Opryland. My dream had ended.

My little daughter Sarah called out my name and came running to me. I took her in my arms and hugged her close. Oh, how I hoped that her memories of home would someday be as dear to her as mine are to me. My dream of home made me want to hold my wife and each of my children close. Life seemed so good.

Each time I have searched for more information about my parents and each time I have written about them, another fiber of love has been woven into my memory of them. Every memory of them has helped me to be more and more grateful that so much of them is within me.

The next time I saw Noel I stated, "Noel, now I know why you spend so much of your time as a heritage hunter."

"Why?"

"You know and I know, but it's hard to put into words." He didn't reply, but we understood each other.

7 *The Search Deepens*

A quick look at my pedigree chart told me that I was in trouble. I had only two parents but I had four grandparents. How would I ever find time to become an authority on each of them? I dialed Noel's number and heard him say, "Hello."

"Noel," I cried out in desperation, "I haven't got time to learn about all of these people."

"Why?" Noel asked. "Are you about to die?"

"I hope not. Why do you ask?"

"Well, you have all the time between now and the time you die to do it. I've told you before that this work is not a summer project; it's a lifelong pursuit." He concluded, "I've got to go now. I'm close to some new information about Christopher."

"Speaking of Christopher, I've been meaning to ask. How could—" The sudden dial tone indicated that Noel had hung up.

I felt better and made a mental note to eat better and exercise more because, at the rate I was going, I would need a long life to complete this work.

The next day I went to Noel's office. While we looked at my pedigree chart, Noel gave me his unfailing advice. "Instead of looking for both sets of grandparents right now, let's just start with the Durrants. He prepared to write the names of my Durrant grandparents on the pedigree chart. "All right, George, the genealogist, what was your grandfather's name?"

Before he looked up, I quietly got up and began to run out of his office. He spied me leaving and shouted, "Hey, wait! I know you don't know, but before you go we need to plan."

I returned sheepishly. I sat back down and he asked, "What do we do first?"

"Well, let's see," I answered, "I do have a manila folder on each of my grandparents, but the folder is a bit thin."

"At least that is a beginning, and we can fatten the folders up." Noel advised me to contact my relatives and seek information from them.

"Do you think they'll help me? They may not be as interested as I am in these things."

"Sure, they'll help, but you have to approach them in the right way."

"How do I do that?"

"Tell them what you're doing and why. Tell them that you will give them a copy of whatever you come up with. If they have a picture, assure them that if they'll let you take it you'll bring back the original plus an extra copy. Always be honest in what you're doing, and they'll trust you and really help you. If you have pictures that they don't have, give them a copy."

Noel continued. "I have a cousin named George, who knew of my interest in our common ancestor. I had given him a number of pictures. One day I was totally shocked by his generosity. He brought me my grandmother's wedding ring and told me he felt I would treasure it, and he wanted me to have it. People will help if you ask them."

During the next few days I followed Noel's suggestion. I called my aunt. She was thrilled that I called. She lived in another state, and I hadn't seen her for years. She chastised me for not coming to see her. She couldn't remember much about her father (my grandfather) because he had died when she was a small girl. She did have some pictures of him which she offered to send to me.

I also drove to the home of my uncle who lived in the same city as I did. It was so good to see Uncle Jim again. He had always been a family hero. He was big and handsome and had been a great football player in his younger days.

He was far happier to see me than I had thought he would be. It seems that as life goes on, we feel closer and closer to our relatives.

I told him that I was seeking information about my Grandfather Durrant. He got out a small pile of pictures. He related to me all that he knew about each picture. I became more and more excited. I hardly dared ask, but I finally did. "Uncle Jim, could I take these pictures and have copies made?"

"Oh, sure," he replied with enthusiasm. "If you are writing something about mom and dad I'll do anything to help you."

He told me a story or two that he could remember about grandfather, but he couldn't remember much because he was a small boy when his father had died.

The visit with Uncle Jim was another pleasant experience. It is amazing how satisfying visits with relatives can be when one is seeking information about ancestors.

Now I had had some success, but not as much as I deserved. I reported to Noel that I wasn't finding out much about my grandparents. He reminded me about what we had found on our visit to American Fork.

"Yes," I replied, "I know what we found there. But I need to find out more than that."

"Be calm," Noel said. "I've got more free time now. I'll help you." The following day during lunch we were at the library looking at microfilms of old newspapers. We found an obituary on my grandfather. It didn't say much, but one line struck deep into my heart: "William was neither prominent in the church or in the community."

I was a little upset about this statement, and I thought, "Well, maybe he wasn't prominent to whoever wrote the obituary, but he sure was prominent to me." I became determined to learn more about him. Often as I walked, shaved, or rode the bus he would pop into my thoughts. He was becoming more and more prominent to me even though I didn't know any more about him because I continually felt more about him.

Every time I looked at his picture I could almost see him come alive. He had somehow established himself as my favorite ancestor. I couldn't explain why, but that is the way I felt and still feel about him.

I visited Delbert Chipman again. He told me that he could not remember my grandfather very well, but he did recall that grandfather had worked on the threshing machine and that he was really a hard worker. "Your grandfather's job included counting the sacks of grain. He never erred in the count. He was a pleasant man and a good, honest, hard-working fellow." That was about all he could remember.

As Noel and I continued our search we found a newspaper article about the death of one of grandfather's children, a young boy named Stewart. The family lived near the railroad tracks, and seven-year-old Stewart had been near the tracks as a train passed by. The boy fell under the train, and his legs were cut off. Grandfather was one of the first at the scene. He held his little son in his arms as the boy died. I was close to tears, but not for Stewart as much as for my grandfather.

I learned that my grandfather had worked at the sugar factory, on farms, and had run a thresher. Those who remembered him reported that he was an excellent gardener and that he knew much about plants, shrubs, and trees.

Using all the information I could find about him, I wrote a short history of my grandfather's life.

In that history I included a story that Uncle Jim had told me:

> As a small child I remember there was a dirt road in front of our house. Much of the time this road was muddy. Each Sunday we children would all get ready

to go to Church. Father wouldn't go, but he would lead us all to the side of the muddy road. Then, one at a time, he would put us up on his shoulders and carry us piggyback across the mud to the dry path on the other side.

I can remember him carrying me on his back as well as if it were yesterday. He did this every time the road was muddy, and when we returned from Church he was always there to carry us back.

As I wrote these words in my grandfather's history, I had a very strange feeling. I could feel my grandfather very near to me. In my heart I heard his voice: "My dear grandson, I hope there is something to make you proud of me because I am deeply proud of you."

Feeling his presence so near to me was an experience I shall never forget. Since then I have often thought that it is important to be proud of our ancestors, but it is even more important to live in such a way as to make our ancestors proud of us.

I can remember my Grandmother Durrant. She is my only grandparent whose earthly life overlapped mine.

During my early teens my grandmother would often ask me, "George, do you have a girl friend?"

I was quite bashful, and I would blush and never answer her. I loved her because she thought I was handsome and would have a lot of girls interested in me. When I related this to Noel, he replied, "She wasn't a very perceptive woman, was she?"

"She was not only perceptive, but she was a good story teller. It was really amusing to listen to her talk. She was a real wit."

"A real wit, you say?" After a pause he added, "It seems she passed just half of that talent on to you."

Noel seemed to be getting the best of me, so I decided to change the tenor of our discussion. "Noel, something very strange and wonderful happened to me last night."

Noel sensed my seriousness. "What was it?"

"I was reading a history of Grandmother Durrant when into my mind came a strong impression. I felt that my Grandmother Mayne wanted me to learn more about herself."

"She's mentioned in your mother's history quite often, isn't she?" Noel asked.

"Yes, she is, and I believe that that's one of the reasons she is on my mind so much."

"Well, you'd better follow the impression. It seems that some of our ancestors almost cry out from the past to be remembered."

"Noel, I feel that so much of what I am came from my mother. She and I were not only mother and son, but we were the closest and most personal friends. What my mother gave to me she received from her mother, so my Grandmother Mayne and I are cut right out of the same cloth."

Noel was silent as I continued. "I was particularly touched by a story that my mother recorded in her history about her mother. Do you remember the one about whistling in heaven?"

"Yes, I remember. Did your Grandmother Mayne write that story?" Noel asked.

"All I know is what my mother told me: 'I don't know if mother wrote this story, but I think she did.' So I suppose that all I can say for certain is that my grandmother loved it enough to memorize it. I love it too. When I see her again in heaven I'll walk toward her whistling a tune."

"Let's see, how did it go?" Noel asked.

"The first portion of the poem describes a young mother who has been left alone with her baby in a frontier cabin. Her husband was on a two-day journey to obtain food. Evening came and she was in terror of being alone. Let's see, it's right here." I read the poem to Noel.

> The darkness of night had fallen,
> And I was so utterly helpless
> With no one in reach of my call.
> There I sat until late in the evening,
> And scarcely an inch did I stir,

When suddenly far in the distance,
The sound of a whistle I heard.
I started up, terribly frightened,
For fear 'twas a red man's call.
And then suddenly I remembered
That red men ne'er whistled at all.
The whistling grew louder and louder,
And then came a soft, gentle knock on the door.
I ran to the door, threw it wide,
And there to my joy and amazement,
A fifteen-year-old boy stood outside.
We gazed at each other a moment,
And before either had time to speak,
I just threw my glad arms around him,
And gave him a kiss on the cheek.
And these are the words that he said:
"Ma'am, we saw your husband go eastward,
And we made up our minds where he'd gone.
And I said to the rest of my people,
'That woman is there all alone,
And I'll bet you she's terribly lonely.
And though she may have no great fear,
I think she would feel a bit safer,
If only a boy were but near.'
So taking my axe on my shoulder,
And wishing to save you alarm,
I whistled a tune just to show you
I didn't intend any harm.
So now here I am at your service,
But if you don't want me to stay,
Why, all you have to do is to say so,
And shouldering my axe I'll away."
I dropped in a chair and near fainted
Just at the thought of his leaving me then,
And his eyes gave a knowing, bright twinkle,
And he said, "Well, I guess I'll remain."
Yes, often I've said so in earnest,
And now these few words I'll repeat,

That unless there's a boy there a-whistling,
Heaven's music will not be complete.

"That's great." Noel's tone was subdued.

"Why do I love her so much, Noel?" I asked. "I hardly knew her until I started thinking of her, and now I feel so close to her. Every time I whistle I can see her in my mind."

Noel and I continued to talk about our ancestors. The tone of our conversation was deeply spiritual. We both agreed that genealogy and studying one's heritage is far more than just a hobby. It's a sacred quest.

"Noel, last night I was reading the newspaper, and I saw a picture of the state mental institution in Provo. The picture was taken in the early 1900s. It revealed a bleak and foreboding institution. I read the account of the treatment received by the mentally ill patients of that day. As I did so I wept inwardly because my mother's history revealed that my grandmother spent many lonely years there.

"It seems that the tragedies of life really loaded her down. Finally it all became too much, and this sensitive woman, my beloved Grandmother Mayne, became ill. After several years in that hospital, she recovered somewhat from her affliction and was able to return home. A few years later she died in her own home in Alpine.

"Noel, I feel that it means much to her that I have remembered her, and because I know you will understand I would just like to say something to her in front of you. Grandmother Mayne, I love you with all my heart. I am deeply proud of you and am grateful to you. I feel so much of you in me, and that which I feel is by far my better part."

"George, you have come a long way," Noel responded. "Your history and ancestral pedigree are adding up inside of you. You have studied, researched, and written, and I can tell that you feel good about what you have done. Now you know that through your ancestors you have become you."

"But I'm not through yet, Noel. The thing I desire to do now is to unravel the mystery that presented itself when you, Stewart, and I visited the American Fork Cemetery.

"Remember, it was there that we found the grave marker of John Durrant, and below his name was listed not one but two wives. Do you feel that John Durrant was a polygamist, Noel?"

"He might have been. Many of the early Mormons were. As a matter of fact, Christopher Layton . . ."

Just at that second the phone rang. Noel picked it up, answered, "Hello" and added, "I'll be right there." He hung up. "I've got to go."

"What were you going to say?" He was out the door by now. "I'll tell you later," he shouted back.

The next day I knocked on Noel's door. "Come in," he called out. After seeing me, he urged, "Come in, I've been waiting for you. Let's get going on John Durrant." While I sat nearby he wrote the name John Durrant on my pedigree chart. Noel really did it with a flourish. Even a seasoned, heritage hunter veteran like Noel was getting excited about stalking the information on such a man. As we sat together in a sort of pre-game huddle, Noel unfolded the game plan.

I mentioned to Noel that I had a relative who, I understood, had spent much time and money working on Durrant genealogy. Noel was excited. "Get her on the phone and make an appointment," he suggested. I did just that, and she graciously agreed to come to my office the next day to meet with Noel and me.

When she arrived she brought much more than we had hoped for. She placed before us a neatly bound set of papers and explained that it was the personal history of John Durrant. He had written it while he was in prison.

"Prison!" I gulped. Noel's eyes opened wide and looked at me as if to say, "Just be quiet and listen."

"Yes, my dear grandfather, and your great-grandfather," she added, "spent several months in the Utah State Prison."

"Was it because he had two wives?" Noel asked.

"No," she answered. "It wasn't because he had two wives — it was because he had three wives."

Noel was puzzled.

"We only saw two on the gravestone."

"Well, if you had looked a little further east, you would have found the grave of Jemima, the third wife." I was both spellbound and speechless.

For more than an hour this dear relative, who I learned was my great-aunt, told us all that she knew about John Durrant. The more she told me about him, the more I loved him. I was pleased to know that this lovely woman and I were from the same wife, Elizabeth Jane Ginger Durrant. My great-grandmother was her grandmother.

After a long visit my great-aunt departed, but she left me the history. I gripped it tightly while traveling home on the bus. Tonight would be a night to remember. I would read the personal history of John Durrant, my great-grandfather.

John recorded that he was born in Bovingdon, Hertfordshire, England. He described his childhood:

> I went to infant school a little while, say a few years, with my sister, Mary, until she was burnt to death in the year 1844, on Feb. fourteenth. She was buried in the Bovingdon Parish churchyard by the side of her brother. She was a good girl and her mother loved her very much.

He also described his home life:

> Bread was very scanty with us, butter put on and then scraped off again.

His father was ill while he was but a boy, forcing John to work to sustain his family. He describes his many childhood jobs. First he labored on a berry farm near his home, and one of his duties was shepherding the sheep. While he was thus employed, his father died. His cruel employer insisted that John stay with the sheep and refused to allow him to attend the funeral.

He wrote of his mother:

> Who can tell what mother had to undergo? I have said many times, "Mother what are you crying for?"

The reply would be, "My boy, the greatest desire I have is to live and see you two youngest boys grow up so that you can both take care of yourselves."

Life went on, and John recalled:

Now I was changed to different work. Called up every morning at three o'clock to help clean the horses and do other things. I worked from three in the morning until eight in the evening for two years. Not only were the hours long, but the employers were often cruel.

He described one of his masters:

For very little frivolous things he would beat us with an easel stick until we were bruised and carried wales for weeks, and all because my father was not alive to protect us."

He wrote of his own free spirit:

He [the master] got drunk one day, came down into the meadow where I was herding the sheep and then found me and his other boy who should have been in another field keeping the crows off the barley and wheat. This boy, Henry Smith, sauced him and ran away. He then caught hold of me and commenced beating me. I took it very mild. Soon after our master had gone home, this boy Smith came to me and said, "I would not stand that if I were you; I would go up and demand my money if I were you. Come on, and I will demand mine too." We both went up to the farmhouse and demanded our money. The mistress paid off Smith and told me I had better go back to the sheep again, but I insisted on her paying me like she had done the other. Mrs. Lines went into the house and told her son that I wouldn't go back. Her son, Thomas, came out of the house saying, "Bring me that rope—I will tie him up to the mill." I took it very patiently, and they tied me to the old mill. They went into the house for a little while, and later they returned. Looking at me, Thomas said, "Will you go back to the sheep if I let you loose?" "No, sir, but I will make you pay pretty dearly for your beating me and tying me to the mill, for I have the marks to show on my back and on my wrists." The old lady, his mother, hearing these words said, "Thomas let the boy loose, and I will pay him if he wants to go." I was soon liberated and free. My mother wanted to know why I was home so early. I told her what had happened. She said, "You had better go back to your work in the morning, for I don't know what we shall do if you don't keep on in your work." But I was willing to search for work somewhere else.

The following reveals more of his personality:

Giles Austin saw me working in our little garden before going to work for him. I suppose he was jealous of me. I left our little garden and went down to the farmhouse; the other men had just gone out of the house to work. I asked him what I was to do today, and he replied that I ought to have been here an hour earlier. Says I, "It is not yet six o'clock—that's the time we should go to work I thought." "Well," says he, "if you are so particular, you had better take your money and go." Says I, "Let me have it. I never refuse taking money, thank-you." He then called me a saucy little devil and told me to go and hoe wheat in Bush field, but I insisted on his paying me off. He then said it was just like me to work for him in the winter, and now that the sun was commenced to shine, wanting to leave him. Says I, "The sun doesn't shine this morning." It was quite a foggy morning. He went off into the fields next and told his son to attend to me.

As I read I thought, *I wish I had said that.*

John Durrant home in Bovingdon, Hertfordshire, England

He recalls that in 1858 he came in contact with a Mormon missionary, and on July of that year he was baptized a member of that faith. This single event changed his entire future. It ultimately placed him in a prison cell in Utah and gave him the time to write his life story.

John recorded that for the next three years he had several jobs. He was a "turnip snouter," a "stubber," and a "grubber." I feel I might have inherited these "grubber," "stubber," and "snouter" talents, or at least I hope I did because they sound like good qualities of success.

It was the custom at that time for new Mormon converts to go to "Zion." (Zion, to them, was in America.) John recorded that he was caught up in this spirit and told his mother so:

> This seemed to grieve her very much but I explained the necessity of "gathering" the best I could.

A few months later he reported:

> I started off for home to get ready to pack my clothes in a box, when my mother said, "Then you intend going, do you?" "Yes, mother, I must go. I have already my certificate in my possession and that says I must be down to Liverpool on the tenth of April, 1861." I bade my sister Charlotte good-bye, and she gave me ten shillings to help me off. They were both crying and said they should never see me or Edward again, for the ship might sink. I told them not to fear, I was in the Lord's hands and he would guide the vessel in all storms and guide me safely through."

He described his sailing:

> April sixteenth, 1861, I started for America on the sailing ship, Manchester, about 11:00 A.M., it being very calm. April seventeenth, still calm weather; April eighteenth, fair sailing.

He listed each day until May 16, 1861, when the ship anchored in New York Harbor. The next night he met his brother, Edward, who had preceded him to America one year earlier. John wrote about this meeting:

> Edward and I laid in the same bed; we were talking about the old country all night. We saw the daylight approaching before we dropped off to sleep.

He later traveled by train and boat and finally was hired out to drive an ox team one thousand miles across the desert to his longed-for Zion.

From this point on I shall retain his original spelling and punctuation which reveals something of his education and accent.

In the fall of 1861 he arrived at his journey's end:

> We started off the next morning October 18, 1861, drove into Salt Lake City the same day I felt very much please to think that God had permitted me to reach my destination in safety.

He told of his inability to handle horses and mechanical things in an experience which occurred shortly after he arrived in Utah:

> Mr. Fisher I will give you ten dollars a money and your board for the winter if you wish to stay with us. I agreed to that bargan and started to work the next morning. October 21st he set me to hall wood from the mountains with a yok of wild stears which he had borrowed from Brother Betrell, and acquaintance of his and a shew maker by trade. I started off with the cettell and a two wheeled cart up the mountains. I could not make them climb up. They got the best of me and ran down the mountain up setting the cart. I concluded to cut som green mapels, load up and go home, which I did. Brother Fisher, my boss concluded he whould not send me again for a

wile. So he sent me down on his sons farm to plow out potatoes.

The came the event that made my heart almost skip a beat when I read the name "American Fork":

> Brother George Palmer drove a team acrost the plains with us and he tried to perswade me to come to American Fork with him but I told him I must go back and get my clothes.

From that day in 1861 until now, the name *Durrant* and the beautiful city of American Fork have been woven together as one unified fabric.

John's ability to grub paid off because he took work grubbing willows in American Fork. He must have accomplished the task well because there are but a few willows left in my hometown.

While visiting in Salt Lake City a few months later, he met Jemima Henson. He later wrote of her:

> I told Br. Biggs that I should hask Jemima to go to American Fork when I whas ready to go. He said I whould do well if I could get her to go with me has a wife for he new her to be a good girl in the old countery. Thinks I to my self that whould sute me if it should so happen. So one evening we whas talking together I hasked her if she should like to go to American Fork to live with us this winter. The reply was ye if you will devide your blankets with me when I get there. Says I if necesity required it I whould. So I concluded to go down to American Fork and get the new room built up ready for Edward and wife, myself and Jemima if she concluded to come.

Later he returned to Salt Lake City on a hopeful mission of getting his bride:

> Now Jemima cherfulle informed me that she had been hearning a wash tub and some other things that whould

be useful in housekeeping. I took it for granted that she ment what she said. Sister Adams enquired of me if I had come to take her hired girl away. I said yes if she was ready; Jemima looked at me with a smile on her countenance saying is the new room ready to move in to. I said no not yet. But we was getting along perty well with it. Edward had been to Provo and got what was due him in lumber. And when I got back we could soon put the flooring down. I also said I thought she had better come and help to fix it so we baid them good by and started for American Fork thirty miles south from Salt Lake City, Nov. 1862. We started on our journey very earley that morning. The wind was blowing very cold so much so that we was compelled to lap the quilts around us to keep warm.

I could just see those two happy people drawn close together under the same blanket, being pulled along by a contented horse who almost knew that he was taking the makings of a whole community of Durrants to their new home.

I smiled, and at the same time almost cried with joy as I considered John's description of his and Jemima's wedding.

Wm. Paxman came down to se how we was getting along and asked me and Jemima to come and eat Christmas dinner with them. We excepted the offer and whent up into his duggout to spend part of Christmas day with them. Hafter eating dinner Bro. Paxman and his wife Ann seemed to be in a real good umer and said to us I don't se why you two don't get married. She laughed and I said there is no one to marrie us as I know of. Bro. Paxman said Bishop Harington will soon come over and marray you if you go over and ask him. I said I did not like to go over to his house. Bro. Paxman and myself left the women in the house whilst we whent out to cut som wood. The bishop soon came along that way to feed his stock. Bro. Paxman said nows your time to ask him. I told him I did not like to but I whent to hask him. And he said yes wheair is she. I shall have to be quick about it for

I've promised to go to a supper tonight. I said she is in Bro. Paxmans house. He said and what is her name. Jemima Henson I replied and is she a Daneish woman. No ser. She is an English woman. He came down into the house and shuck hands with us all. And asked Jemima is she whas willing to be married to Bro. John. She smiled and said yes. But I did not know that he was going to fetch you hear now for that purpas. He then asked me if I whas willing to take Jemima Hinson to be my lawful and wedded wife. I said yes. He then and their pronounced the seremony and told us to kiss each other and we did.

So John and Jemima were married. About the time John finished this story during his imprisonment, the warden must have beckoned him and told him he was free.

Oh, if he could have only stayed in prison a little longer! Then I could have known about the rest of his life.

The next night Noel read John Durrant's history. He was almost as excited as I was, but, of course, no one else could be as excited about my own ancestor as I was.

Now that Noel knew my ancestor had been in prison, he suggested that we go to the prison and look at the records. The next day Noel and I entered Utah State Prison—just on a visit, of course. We parked the car and passed the guard tower. We entered the front office and asked to see the prison records. At first we were told that they didn't have any such records, but Noel persisted. Finally we were led to a room and shown some old books that dated back to the prison's origin. As the door clanked behind us, we saw the records on a table before us. We were in heaven within a prison!

We each looked at several books. Finally Noel shouted, "Here it is!" He read aloud as we both looked:

(Prisoner) John Durrant (Court) 1st District Court (Crime) U.[nlawful] C.[ohabitation] (Sentence) From Oct. 21st 1886 (6) Six months $100 fine, no costs. Hold until paid. (Date of Confinement) Oct. 21st 1886 (Occupation) Laborer (Complexion) Dark (Age) 46 (Height) 5'4½" (Eyes) Dark Brown (Hair) Dark (Other Distinctive Marks) England, 155# (Remarks) Released under Copper Act March 20th, 1887 on payment Fine and Costs.

I could hardly believe my eyes. I had accepted the fact that he had been in prison, but seeing the actual prison record of the event made it seem dramatically real.

We continued reading to see who else had been in prison at the same time. There were murderers, horse thieves, and robbers. After several more minutes of searching, Noel shouted, "Hey look! Here's John Durrant again. He must have been in here twice."

We looked together as Noel read:

(Prisoner) John Durrant (Court) 1st District Court (Crime) Unlawful Cohabitation (Sentence) From 29 Sept. 1888, 18 months (Date of Confinement) 29 Sept. 1888 (Occupation) Gardener (Complexion) Dark (Age) 52 (Height) 5'4½" (Eyes) Brown (Hair) Black (Other Distinctive Marks) England, 150# (Remarks) Temperate, can read and write, discharged 14 Dec. 1889, Copper Act.

We compared the dates and, sure enough, he had been in prison a second time. I became excited. "In his writings he seemed like a persistent person, and here is proof that he didn't give up easily." We surmised that after his original release, he persisted in his polygamy practice and was sent to prison a second time.

As Noel and I drove away from the prison, we felt like detectives who had just solved a crime. However, so much of the mystery of John Durrant was yet to be unwoven.

In the days that followed I didn't have to pester Noel. He pestered me. He had smelled the scent and wanted to find more.

While in the library, we found newspaper accounts of John's arrest, trial, and incarceration. We read of the sentencing of John Durrant and other American Fork polygamists.

The accounts were brief.

Deseret Evening News - 20 April 1886
An Extensive Haul: By special dispatch just received from American Fork we learn that four well-known and highly respected residents of that place - Samuel Wagstaff, W. R. Webb, John Durrant and John P. Kelly were arrested for unlawful cohabitation this morning early by deputies Vandercook, Redfield, Glen, Smith and Doyle. Wm. Duncan acting as spotter.

The prisoners will be brought to this city this evening.

Deseret Evening News - 8 Oct. 1886
There was not much going on in the First District Court on Wednesday or Thursday. The grand jury reported five indictments - two United States and three Territorial.

Yesterday afternoon the case of the United States vs. John Durrant, of American Fork, indicted for unlawful cohabitation, was called.

Deseret Evening News - 22 October 1886
To the "pen.": Last evening the following brethren were brought from Provo and taken to the penitentiary to serve out their terms of imprisonment for refusing to renounce their wives.

The article named John Durrant and three others.
We visited the Utah State archives collection to find an account of the court proceedings but found nothing. Noel wrote to the Archives Branch of the Denver Federal Records Center, and in a few weeks we were thrilled to receive the account of that trial.
We visited the State Capitol building and searched through the military records. I was thrilled to find that John Durrant had fought in the Indian Wars.

Later we went to the Bureau of Vital Statistics and received a copy of John's death certificate.

In the special collections section in the LDS Church Historical Department library, we found an account book of the John Durrant Molasses Company in American Fork. As I held that book in my hands I felt the reality of my great-grandfather. "Noel, just think, this is the very account book of his business."

These discoveries had taken time. There is still much to learn about John Durrant. Noel and I are still looking. We have plans to search various records in England such as parish registers, bishops' transcripts, census records, poor-law records, probate records, and many others. We both know that somewhere in some record there is information that will reveal more about this persistent, deeply devoted religious man who had left the old world and come to his Zion.

One day as Noel and I were having lunch together, I confided, "I can feel John Durrant's blood in my veins. I long to be as devoted, persistent, and unwavering as he was."

"I know what you mean," Noel replied. "I feel the same way about Christopher Layton."

Hearing the name Christopher Layton caused my mind to focus on an old question. "Noel, you told me once that that great man was both your great-great-grandfather and your great-grandfather.

"That's right." Noel had a smile on his face and a twinkle in his eye.

"How could he be?"

"Well, George, it's like this. Christopher had ten wives."

"Ten wives!" I shouted so loudly that three people at the next table almost choked on their spaghetti.

"Keep your voice down," Noel whispered. "Yes, he had ten wives and sixty-five children. Now, this is how he became my double ancestor.

"My great-great-grandmother on my father's side was his third wife. My great-grandmother on my mother's side was his tenth wife. So you see, he is both my great-great grandfather through my father and my great-grandfather through my mother. Now can you see how it works?"

"Well, I suppose so." I was still a bit confused. Then I thought a bit more.

"Yes, I can see it, I think. Maybe that explains why you are twice as good at genealogy as I am," I replied admiringly.

8   *Information Unlimited*

T he phone was already ringing as I walked into my office
 the next morning. I hurriedly threw my overcoat at a
hanger, lunged across my desk chair for the phone and
shouted, "Hello."

"It's about time you were getting to work." The voice was
unmistakable.

"Good morning, Noel." I wondered why he was calling
me so early.

"How would you like to see one of the wonders of the
world?" he asked.

"I'd like to," I replied, "but I've already seen you before."

"Thank you." I thought he spoke a little skeptically. "But
this time it isn't me. As you know, right here in Salt Lake City
is the great genealogical library of The Church of Jesus Christ
of Latter-day Saints. Meet me at the main entrance at noon,
and we'll spend our lunch hour there."

"But when will I eat?" I waited for an answer, but Noel
had hung up.

The morning seemed to pass quickly. At the appointed time I hurried to the library. I didn't want to be late. Noel didn't like people to be late, unless of course it was one of his "late" ancestors.

As I entered the library I saw Noel waiting inside. I sensed that he was really at home there. On the other hand, the library made me feel uncomfortable. I had been there before, but because I didn't understand the numbering system used to organize the material the place sort of frightened me.

"Welcome to one of the wonders of the world." Noel smiled and shook my hand. "Did you bring some paper?" I held up a yellow pad. "Good," he responded. "You've got to have paper when you come here."

We hurried toward the many small drawers that made up the huge card catalogue. "We'll have to hurry." Noel pulled open a drawer which was labeled "Hertfordshire, England."

He handed me the drawer. "Find Bovingdon; that's where John Durrant was born."

I thumbed through the cards. "Here it is."

"Write down the call number."

I did, and Noel put the drawer back and hurried off. "Come on, we must hurry."

We took a crowded elevator to the fourth floor. Noel asked several of the people where they were from. "New York," "British Columbia," and "Scipio" came the answers.

The door opened and Noel exited. "This is the British Reference Area." I followed my fast-moving companion, trying not to crash into any of the various people hurrying to and fro. I was amazed by the many rows of microfilm reading machines, each occupied by an eager researcher.

Soon Noel had led me to row after row of metal file cabinets containing film. He read the many numbers on the cabinets. "Here it is." He pulled open a drawer. "What is the exact number?" he asked.

"It's 596,744," I replied, pleased that I was helping.

Noel plucked out one of the hundred little white boxes. "Let's find a reader," he instructed as he closed the drawer and walked away. On the other side of the library we found one that was unoccupied. Noel gave me the box. "Thread the film."

I held the roll of microfilm in my hand. I was a bit confused, for I had never been very good with audiovisual equipment. Noel kindly gave me a few instructions, and soon the film was in the machine, the light was on, and there before my eyes were the words, "Bishop's Transcript, 1604 to 1850, Bovingdon, Hertfordshire, England."

"This film contains all the christenings, marriages, and burials in the Bovingdon Parish from 1604 to 1850," my teacher announced.

"You mean, I might find the actual christening record of my great-grandfather, John Durrant?"

"That's right. Move the film to the year 1837. That's the year John was born."

My hand trembled with anticipation as I moved the film forward until that date appeared.

"Slow down!" Noel cautioned excitedly.

The original transcript from which the film was made was old and quite decayed. Some of it seemed to be unreadable. Noel was concerned. "This is bad. I hope John's entry will be legible."

I was almost panicky as I saw the condition of the record get worse and worse as we searched for the year we needed. Then I had a most unforgettable thrill. "There!" I shouted, "Noel, that's it! That's it!"

Before my eyes lay the photograph of a partially decayed page. The borders of the original document were gone, but the information was legible: "ohn, son of William and Mary Durrant of Bovingdon, father a laborer." The "J" was missing, but this was my John.

"That's him." Noel was proud to have helped me.

Suddenly, my mind went back one hundred and forty-two years, and I could see my beloved great-grandfather as a little baby.

"Noel, this is one of the greatest experiences of my life. This is a photo of the actual record. Look at the handwriting of the minister. I wonder what he was like."

"Let's carefully copy down what it says, exactly as it is on the film," Noel instructed. "Then we can look for other members of the family."

"Hey, look," he added, "there is his sister Mary in the entry right above his. They were christened on the same day. Let's see, she was two years old at the time."

For the next few minutes I was in a different world. We found many Durrants. Somehow I usually spotted them before Noel did. The name Durrant seemed to jump right out at me.

As we searched through the precious film we found other Durrant children: Edward, Joseph, Sarah, Henry, James, and finally Charlotte. I carefully wrote down all the details we found.

While looking at the deaths, we found that Mary had died at age five. "I remember John mentioning that in his history," I commented to Noel in the sad tone that comes when considering the death of a child. We also found that James had died at age fifteen.

We discovered that my great-great-grandfather, William, had died at age fifty in 1847. "Could we find his christening?" I asked excitedly.

"Probably," Noel answered. "Move the film back to the year 1797." Sure enough, there it was on October 22, and again I felt a thrill. We also found the christening of Mary Stewart, daughter of Josiah and Mary Stewart.

Would Josiah and Mary Stewart be my great-great-great-grandparents?" I asked.

"That's right."

What a thrill! My heart was filled with love for these people who had suddenly come alive.

"We'd better move on," Noel urged. "We have other information to find."

I put the film back in the box. "This is priceless, Noel."

As we returned the film I felt as if I had discovered a new world. "I can't believe it, Noel. Why didn't you bring me here before?"

"I wanted to save this until last. I wanted you to know that you can find things about your family in many ways. I was afraid that if I brought you here first you would never have wanted to go anyplace else."

"That's understandable. This place is indeed a wonder of the world."

Noel hurried off in another direction. "Let me show you something else." He seized a book entitled, *Index to Civil Registrations of Births, Marriages and Deaths for England and Wales.* "We will look for the name Elizabeth Jane Ginger, John's second wife and your great-grandmother."

We found what we needed in the index, and we were soon picking up another film. We threaded it into the machine and found the name of my great-grandmother in the index. I copied the information carefully: Elizabeth Jane Ginger, WATFORD Vol. 3a, page 270."

"Now if you want," Noel explained, "you can send to St. Catherine's House in London and get a copy of her birth certificate."

We decided not to look in the probate records for Durrants. Noel thought that because the Durrants appeared to be so poor, they probably didn't have much property to be probated. I questioned the possibility that the Durrants of Bovingdon were poor because they couldn't have been more important to me had they all been millionaires — at least, I couldn't have loved them more if they had been.

Next we viewed a film of the 1851 census. We found the following in the Bovingdon parish:

> 38 Bridge Row: Eliza Stewart, head of house, straw plaitter
> John Durrant, cousin, age 13, ag.[ricultural] lab.-[orer] boy
> Edward Durrant, cousin, age 14, ag. lab. boy

"It appears that the boys lived away from their mother," I noticed sadly.

"It looks that way," Noel replied.

Somehow it seemed that we were experiencing now what had happened to these people over one hundred years ago. As we moved the film forward in the machine we found this entry:

> St. Collins Farm, Samuel Phillips, head of household,
> farmer of 80 acres, employing six laborers
> [Ten others were listed, and then:]
> Mrs. Durrant, servant, widow, 50 years old

I felt like crying. My dear great-great-grandmother was living apart from her children, as a servant.

In the 1861 census we found that Mary was now working as a straw plaitter and that John, her twenty-three-year-old unmarried son, was living with her.

In the emigration index we found the name John Durrant. We looked at another film and found that John had sailed from England on the good ship *Manchester*. The journey had begun on April 16, 1861, and he arrived in New York on May 15 of that same year. The cost had been three pounds and sixteen shillings.

I looked at my watch and discovered that it was nearly three o'clock. "Noel, this has been an amazing three hours!"

"We could spend weeks in here," he announced. "We've just scratched the surface of what can be found."

"Are records from other areas of the world as plentiful as the records of England?" I asked.

"Yes, the records from Germany, Scandinavia, other European countries, and the United States, and Canada are good too. There are over a million rolls of microfilm in this library. That's equivalent to some five million books. It has been estimated that there are over a billion names here."

"What if the records weren't here? What would people do then?"

"Well, they could do what I did."

"What was that?" I eagerly awaited the answer from this amazing man.

"Go to the country concerned and go right to the old churches, the county offices, and other places."

"You mean you went to England?"

"Five times," he grinned.

"Five times?" I was surprised. "What did you do?"

"I was there for months at a time. I visited all sorts of old churches, county record offices, homes of relatives all over England, and the Public Record Office, Somerset House, and other places in London."

"What is Somerset House?" I asked.

"It used to be where the birth, marriage, and death records were kept, but now they have been moved to St. Catherine's House."

"It would really be a thrill to go to the places where your own ancestors lived."

"It sure is, but you've done the same thing."

"I have?"

"Sure, you went to American Fork, didn't you?"

"Oh yes, but I was thinking of England."

"When you go to the very place where your ancestors once lived, you can talk to relatives and other people and find documents, family history records, and pictures. I remember talking to a ninety-nine-year-old lady in Northamptonshire who knew some of my ancestors; she gave me a lot of information. I also visited the hamlet where Christopher Layton was born. It hasn't changed much since he lived there. I also visited the church where he was christened."

"I'd love to go to Kings Langley and Bovingdon," I sighed, almost enviously.

"Save your money, George. Save your money."

As we parted Noel observed, "Well, you didn't get any lunch, did you?"

"No, I didn't, but I sure did get full."

"Well, now that you know how to use the library you won't need me anymore. From now on you will be known as George the Genealogist." With that he departed.

As I watched him go the phrase echoed in my mind: "George the Genealogist." That name filled my soul with pride.

At that instant a lady I had never met greeted me: "Hello. I'm from Boston. I'm here to do my genealogy. Could you tell me how to begin?"

I frantically looked for Noel, but he was gone. I stuttered, "Well a . . . let's see . . . you, er . . . ."

I regained my composure. With a calm voice I answered her question. "Just go right in there and talk to the lady at the desk. She'll help you."

"Oh, thank you," she gratefully replied, before she hurried away. I could tell that she had been impressed with "George the Genealogist."

9   *Case Still Open*

S ome time had passed since I last saw Noel. Then one
   morning while seated in my office, I heard a knock on my
door. Somehow I knew before I said, "Come in," that it would
be Noel.

I've never seen him smile with more enthusiasm than he
did as he placed a manuscript in front of me. "I've found some
more material on Christopher which I'm about ready to pre-
pare for publication."

We spent many pleasure-filled moments looking at pictures and reading about his mighty ancestor. The entire time
Noel remained standing and I was seated. He didn't mind,
because when it came to talking about Christopher Layton,
Noel always felt like standing up.

"Well, that's it!" Noel exclaimed as he turned the final
page. "What do you think?"

"Noel, I think it's wonderful," I replied with admiration.
"I love to hear you talk about your ancestors. It gives me a
feeling of deep satisfaction.

"Have you got just a few minutes, Noel? I want to tell
you something that is in the bottom of my heart."

"Sure I've got time."

"Sit down, Noel." I pointed to a nearby chair. I turned my chair toward his, and for just a moment I looked into his eyes.

"Noel, I want to thank you for what you've done for me."

Noel interrupted. "I didn't do anything. You did it yourself."

"Just let me finish, Noel. You've opened the door to a whole new dimension of my thinking. Somehow you've helped me begin to know myself, and even though I can't put it in words you have given me a sort of secure, grateful, warm feeling."

Noel was silent now, and I believe he sensed that I was speaking from the inner reaches of my soul.

I smiled and continued. "I suppose my only real regret about this entire experience is that the one thing I really wanted to find we never did find."

"What's that?" he asked, as if he was eager to start a new search.

"Well, it's something that really doesn't exist anymore."

"What? It might exist. You never know."

"It's almost too personal to mention."

"No, go on and tell me. We'll try to find it."

"All right, I'll tell you. But you must promise me you won't tell anyone else."

"I promise. What is it?" Noel leaned forward in his chair.

"It's my old red school sweater with the white stripe and the big letter *A*.

Noel sort of slumped back in his chair. Then he smiled. "I guess something that old would be gone forever."

"But Noel, in a way I did find it. I found it and the old mill lane and the fish and my school and my mom and dad and my ancestral family!"

I paused. Noel was silent too.

"Nothing really ever goes away, does it Noel?"

"I guess as long as it's something that we love and that we remember it will be with us forever."

"Oh, Noel, I loved that sweater. I wore it with such pride." The speed of my voice quickened with enthusiasm. "I wish you could have seen me in it. I looked magnificent!"

"Maybe you looked just like your wife said you looked when you were younger."

"What did she say?" I asked, fishing for a compliment.

"She said that you weren't pretty and you weren't ugly. You were sort of in between. You were pretty ugly."

Without laughing, I continued. "Seriously, Noel, that sweater is sort of a symbol to me. I wanted so much to grow when I was a boy, and I couldn't seem to. Then one summer I really did grow. Walt Devey had to get me a new sweater because I had grown so much. And somehow I feel that what you and I have done together has made me grow again in an equal but different way. Somehow my soul seems enlarged, and the sweater I wear in my heart still fits."

"Noel, I'm so proud of my ancestors, and looking for my old red sweater seemed to be the event that got me started. I almost tremble when I realize that previously I didn't even know the names of these dear people. Now I feel about them as you can only feel about your own family. Just thinking of John Durrant, my great-grandfather, causes a surge of love and respect to come into my mind. I can see him as he was.

"The other day a relative of mine told me, 'I've been reading Great-grandfather John Durrant's history. I've never seen a picture of him, but as I read I kept thinking that he must have looked just like you.' I corrected her. 'Oh, no, he didn't look like me at all.' "

Noel smiled. "The pictures I've seen of him didn't look like you at all. He was quite handsome!"

I wasn't sure what Noel meant by that. "Yes, he was handsome," I replied. "And he was short, and I'm tall."

I paused and smiled. "But you know, Noel, I can see myself in him. He's sort of a hero to me, and I guess the fact is I want to be like him. Maybe after all it isn't height or shape that makes us look alike. Maybe it's what we are that makes us look alike. Do you know what I'm saying?"

"I'm not sure I know what you're saying, but I think I know what you're thinking."

"Anyway, I've never felt more complimented than when my relative said that she imagined that John Durrant looked like me. Noel, he was really great in my book."

"You mean you're writing a book about him as I am about Christopher?"

Noel's words struck me like a bolt of lightning. "A book on John Durrant! What an idea!" If anyone ever deserved to be the subject of a book, it was my great-grandfather. I'd like to toot his horn for the entire world to hear. I could tell of his spunk, his courage, his wit, his charm, his ambition, his courtship, his marriage, his marriage, his marriage!

Noel smiled.

"Noel, how can we ever do as much for those who come after us as our ancestors did for us?"

Without giving him a chance to reply I continued: "And then there was my dear friend and grandfather, William Durrant. If I could talk to only one of my ancestors it would be him."

Noel seemed to be enjoying my tooting the family horn. He could see that I had ancestor fever. He leaned forward and smiled. "What would you tell him?"

"I'd begin by saying, 'Grandfather, you are my favorite. Why is it that I love you so? I am told you were not prominent among those of your day. What really did you achieve? You don't have to answer now, or even when we meet. Just to have won for yourself the feelings I have for you is achievement enough.

" 'Whatever you did or didn't do, I want you to know that I understand. You were sort of in the middle, weren't you? Your father struggled and traveled and was imprisoned for his faith. You were born and died without ever going as far as the horizon.

" 'While your father was imprisoned you were at home, perhaps wondering why. It's so hard to understand such things when you're young.

" 'As life passed beneath your feet little opportunity seemed to come your way. There was no new faith to accept, for that was already done. There was no school to attend because poverty blocked you from such opportunity. There was no new land to seek because you had your everlasting home. So you worked here and there doing this and that, and while doing so you lived, loved and married, and had a family. Your early death implies that perhaps your health was a problem, but at the same time I am told that you were a vigorous worker. So maybe your health was good. I just don't know. There is so much about you that I don't know.

" 'I have an eight-year-old son. His name is Mark. I love him as you loved your little son, Stewart. That's why I cried inside when I read how you held little Stewart in your arms as he died. You weren't to blame for his playing near the train tracks, but I'm sure you thought you were—and I'm sure you never got over it.

" 'I can see the children on your back as you carry them across the muddy road. I can even see myself on your back reaching down and touching your hair. You would have carried me had I been there, wouldn't you?

" 'I have known many of your children. I have known most of them the way a little boy knows someone who is older. They were all blessed with ambition and honesty. You and grandmother did a good job. You must have been a fine teacher. I have seen pictures of you, but somehow I knew how you looked long before I saw the pictures.

" 'Once while I was thinking of you, you came so near to me, didn't you? Thank you for the pride I could feel that you had in me. I will do all I can to justify that pride. Please don't tell my other ancestors, but you are my favorite. God bless you forever, my grandfather. I will strive to be as unprominently prominent as you were.' "

Noel had listened to my words as only a true friend can. He had invited me to unlock my heart, and I had done so.

"So that's what you'd say?" he asked.

"That's what I'd say."

Noel never misses an opportunity. "You ought to say the same thing in writing. William deserves a book too.

"Think of how honored your Grandmother Mayne would be to see her name on the title of a book, *The Life Story of Estella Jeanette Bateman Mayne*. What would you say to her if you could?" Noel invited.

I sat back in my chair, looked out of the window for a second or two, and then looked back at Noel. "I'd say, 'Grandmother Mayne, you and I both know that when I began this project with Noel we were going to concentrate on Durrants. You aren't a Durrant, nor did you marry a Durrant. I only got started on you because you asked me to and because you're so much in my heart.

" 'You hoped there would be whistling in heaven, and because of that when I come I will whistle. That way you'll know it's me. Of course, you'll know me anyway because there is so much of you in me. You won't know me by the way I look but by the way I feel. After all, it is the way I feel that is really me.' "

"You could title the book about her *Whistler's Grandmother*," Noel suggested with a smile. While I was trying to figure out what he meant, he added, "Your mother already wrote a book about her life, so you would not need to write her book."

"I'd write a preface to her book, Noel."

"What would you say?"

"I'd say, 'Mom, you were my sculptor. You molded me. I would have been so different without you. I could have gone down roads of regret, but you stood at each crossroad. You held a peanut butter sandwich in one hand and with the other you pointed the way. You left me with little choice of direction. Yes, I could have gone the other way, and for a little while I did. But I couldn't go far without running back, kissing you on the cheek, and hurrying in the direction you pointed.

" 'You made a mighty mark in the city, in the Church, in the family, and most of all in my heart. I believe you didn't know, even in part, how everyone loved and respected you.

" 'The pride that you had in me was the greatest motivation in my life. I will have reflections of you in my heart forever. Never will a day go by without my seeing you. You and I are truly as one.' "

"You're pretty good at saying things," Noel responded. "Maybe I ought to get you to write a preface for my book about Christopher Layton."

I could tell he was just kidding, but I felt honored anyway.

"I guess if you wrote all those books, it would take you quite a bit of time," Noel observed.

"It sure would, but they are written in my heart already. I could especially write a lot about my father. He gave me a million memories. What a father he was!"

Noel stood up. "I've been here too long. I have another appointment."

As he went toward the door I felt that I would not see him much anymore. "Noel, is this the end?" I sadly wondered.

"No, George. There is no end."

The door was closed, and Noel was gone. I looked down at my desk and I saw that this great man had left a silver pen.

I picked it up and looked at my distorted reflection. Somehow I didn't feel alone. I wrote with the pen as I spoke in a soft but audible voice.

"So, my dear ancestors, here I sit looking into the reflections of the past. I have no red sweater to wear, for it is gone forever. Yet, somehow I still look or at least feel good. For now that I know you, for the first time I know myself.

"I can't deceive you now, for you are beyond ever being deceived again. Thus, you know that I am totally sincere when I say thank you for being that noble body of people who make up my chain back to the beginning.

"In the years that I have left, I humbly hope that I will stand before you as one in whom you can each have pride — not the pride that comes when one is related to someone who is prominent, but the pride that comes when you see that I have a quiet, sincere appreciation and love for you.

"I shall keep learning of you. I shall strive to put into words my reflection which I am blessed to see. The words on the paper will never adequately describe the feelings that the memories and the knowledge of you put into my heart.

"May the God who created us all someday bring us all together as one big and wonderful family. Until then just let me say, I love you all."

Noel was right. There is no end.